The Truth About Weight Control

How to Lose Weight *Permanently*

NEIL SOLOMON, M.D., Ph.D.
with SALLY SHEPPARD

day books

A Division of
STEIN AND DAY/Publishers/New York

To my loving wife, Frema, and our three lovable sons, Ted, Scott, and Clifford—who each turn me on in his own way

—N.S.

and

to Roger.

—S.S.

FIRST DAY BOOKS EDITION 1981

First Published in hardcover by
Stein and Day/*Publishers*

Stein and Day/*Publishers*
Scarborough House
Briarcliff Manor, N.Y. 10510

Acknowledgments

It would be difficult to name all the people who so generously contributed their time and effort to this undertaking. Busy members of the medical profession, both researchers and practicing physicians, have unstintingly given of their time, and released new data to me. Many others, through their published findings, have also contributed to the fund of knowledge and understanding of the problems confronting the overweight and obese patient.

Although I cannot name every individual who contributed to this effort, I would especially like to thank:

Ronald A. Arky, M.D.; Gordon J. Azar, M.D.; Broda O. Barnes, M.D.; Walter L. Bloom, M.D; Buris R. Boshell, M.D.; Colonel Edwin M. Bradley, M.D.; George A. Bray, M.D.; Thomas A. Burch, M.D.; Bacon F. Chow, Ph.D.; Ernest J. Drenick, M.D.; C. Wesley Dupertuis, Ph.D.; Helen Stimson Dupertuis; Seymour K. Fineberg, M.D.; Ronald McG. Harden, M.B.; Herman K. Hellerstein, M.D.; Jules Hirsch, M.D.; Edward S. Horton, M.D.; A. M. Hsueh, Ph.D.; William McK. Jeffries, M.D.; Alan Kekwick, M.D.; Arthur Kornhaber, M.D.; Alfredo Lopez-S., M.D., Ph.D.; George V. Mann, M.D., Sc.D.; Jean Mayer, Ph.D.; Max Miller, M.D.; Mary B. McCann, M.D., Ph.D.; Irving B. Perlstein, M.D.; Roy F. Roddam,

M.D.; Harold Rosen, M.D., Ph.D.; Stanley Schachter, Ph.D.; A. T. W. Simeons, M.D.; Maria Simonson, Ph.D.; Ethan A. H. Sims, M.D., Malcom C. Smith, Ph.D.; Theodore B. van Itallie, M.D.; Roger J. Williams, Ph.D., Sc.D., and Marjorie C. Zukel, M.P.H.

In addition, Mrs. Beatrice Weitzel CPS, Mrs. Patricia Hosey, Mrs. Gloria Ward, Mrs. Rose Marie Brooks, and Mrs. Lorraine Villeck, my secretaries, and Mrs. Mary Carroll, secretary to Mrs. Sheppard. They have worked tirelessly and selflessly to meet the necessary deadlines and we offer our profound thanks.

I would especially like to thank my wife, Frema, and Mr. George Caldwell for their editorial comments.

The Truth About Weight Control

The Truth About Weight Control will answer hundreds of dieter questions about subjects such as these:

- I eat less than my husband, but I still get fat. Is this medically possible?
- Can diet pills, diet shots, and crash diets such as the "high protein" and "low carbohydrate" diets be dangerous?
- Will losing my excess fat increase my sex drive?
- Do I have to give up eating in restaurants in order to stay on my diet?
- Is exercise important? What exercises are best?
- Is it true that fat parents usually produce fat children?
- If I have gained and lost weight all of my life (the Yo-Yo Syndrome), is it possible to stabilize my weight?

Also included in the book are:

- 13 points you can follow to begin taking off fat right away.
- 2 simple tests you can take at home to determine your individual ideal weight and whether your body contains excess fatty deposits.

Contents

I

Can I Lose Weight and Keep It Off?

"I eat no more than my husband but I gain weight while he does not. Why, Doctor? Is there hope for me?"

This single question was posed most frequently of the fifty most commonly asked by over one thousand patients seen during my ten-year study of permanent weight loss.

The study originated in 1961, during my internship and residency training on the Metabolic Research Ward of the Osler Medical Service of Johns Hopkins Hospital, and has continued up through the present time as I continue to follow some of these private-research patients.

During this decade, these patients have collectively lost—and kept off—over two tons of body fat and they all had one thing in common—they were all metabolically different. That is, they were unique in the way each burned his food, converted it to energy and used this energy for daily functions: working, talking, reproducing, and living.

The answers to those fifty most frequently asked questions will be found as you read through this book. In the following chapters, I will share with you the many problems and their solutions in the hope that this factual presentation will help you scientifically to lose weight permanently.

2

Instant Beginnings, or, What You Can Do Right Now

How can I begin to lose weight even before I make an appointment with my doctor?

As you are reading this book, you can begin to lose weight. Just do the following:

1. Chew all foods very slowly.
2. Do not snack between meals or after dinner.
3. Drink one eight-ounce glass of *ice* water five minutes before beginning each meal.
4. Eat half-portions of whatever you would normally eat, except:
5. Eat no desserts;
6. Drink no alcohol;
7. Use no salt from the shaker at the table.
8. Take a walk beginning one half-hour after each meal.
9. In the morning, prepare a generous supply of emergency foods. Include raw vegetables of your choice such as celery stalks, carrot sticks, radishes, cucumbers, etc. This supply is for any emergency craving later in the day.
10. If your hunger persists after you have eaten the prepared emergency foods, eat these vegetables along with an eight-ounce glass of *ice* water.

11. If the craving continues, take a five-minute walk.
12. If this does not work, try a warm shower.
13. Keep a written diary of everything you take into your mouth—noting the amount and kind of food and drink —and analyze your diary each day—with particular attention to the time of day you overindulged and what triggered you to respond by eating.

I eat many meals in a restaurant. Can I start my diet while I eat out and enjoy it?

Yes. Some tricks while eating out will help you begin and stay on your diet.

I agree that it is difficult at best to start or continue on a diet while eating in restaurants—either full time, once a day, or even occasionally. However, it can be done. I have listed here a few suggestions and ideas that may make it easier for you to stay on your diet but still enable you to enjoy dining out.

Think of your calories as you would a bank balance. You have so many to "spend" per day, so plan exactly how you can use them most effectively. For example, if you know you are going out to dinner, save up some of your calories and make that dinner your only good meal for the day. If you still go over your allotted amount, compensate for this the next day by cutting your calorie quota.

When ordering occasional rich foods, eat only small portions, but eat slowly. Savor these foods and enjoy thoroughly the small amount to which you treat yourself.

It is not only embarrassing, but many times impossible to get diet salad dressing in a restaurant; yet nothing tastes flatter than a salad without the extra snap added by the dressing. Instead of requesting a low-calorie salad dressing, ask for one made from Dijon mustard and lemon juice. Most restaurants will gladly comply with your request, and your salad will be a real treat. You can also ask for your vegetables without butter and your meats *au jus*, without gravy.

Memorize the approximate caloric values of foods which you especially like, and order accordingly. If one of your favorites is very high in calories, then compensate by ordering accompanying dishes which are low in caloric content, or omit altogether some of the usual condiments.

What low-calorie foods can I order? I often frequent French restaurants.

The following are suggested low-calorie foods which you can order when dining out:

APPETIZERS

1. Oysters and Clams. (Watch oysters—they are high in cholesterol but are all right occasionally.)
2. Shrimp. (Occasionally—they are high in cholesterol too.)
3. Raw bay scallops with lemon and freshly ground pepper.
4. Crabmeat with lemon and freshly ground pepper or pimiento.
5. In French restaurants:
   An artichoke with mustard and lemon juice.
   Tomato-and-cucumber salad.
   Peppers with anchovies without oil.

SOUPS

Stick to the clear variety and add no salt.

1. Chicken broth or consommé.
2. Tomato Madrilène.
3. Jellied bouillon.

ENTREES

Watch yourself because the main dishes in restaurants are usually large. Request small portions, and ask that sauces and gravies be omitted.

1. Any grilled or roasted meat is best.
2. Boiled beef or *pot au feu.*
3. Poached chicken and broth or *poule au pot.*

4. *Lean* corned beef with plain steamed or boiled cabbage.
5. Kidneys—broiled—or a combination of sweetbreads and kidneys (these are high in cholesterol too, but all right occasionally) alternated on a skewer with lemon, mustard, or chutney.
6. Rare roast lamb.

DESSERTS

If you are really serious about your diet, skip dessert. However, if you have saved sufficient calories from your meal, fruit makes the best choice.

Beware of the extras such as butter, rolls, and crackers. I have known dieting couples who ask the waiter to leave these tempters off the table. Also watch out for salad which has rich, gooey dressing.

If you have been conscientious and successful in banking your calories, and you find that you have a few extras, the following foods make palate-pleasing rewards.

1. A generous helping of caviar.
2. A thin slice of smoked salmon.
3. A tiny broiled or roast squab, pheasant, or quail, without sauce.

Let your conscience be your guide and keep your calorie count up to date at all times. But by all means keep it out of sight too! It is easier and more enjoyable for you and everyone else if you are simply judicious in ordering, and no one suspects you are giving up a thing.

I don't attend elegant French restaurants. I am just a plain housewife who is overweight. Any practical suggestions?

First and foremost, eat only when you are hungry. When you do eat, sit down at the table and relax. Put small portions of food on your plate. Cut the food into small pieces. Chew each piece thoroughly. Try not to have second helpings. By eating slowly, you will be able to more easily determine when you have had enough. When you feel you have had enough, stop eating and leave the table. Go to another room. If there is still food on your plate, save it to snack on or for another meal or for another day.

It is important to keep low calorie foods in readiness for the times when you really feel you must eat in between meals. Buy tomato juice and bottles of seltzer and keep them in the refrigerator, so you will see them when you go hunting for something to satisfy you. Squeeze some lemon juice in the soda water for variety. Have a pitcher of tea brewed with mint or spices in the refrigerator in the summer. Experiment with various brews, English and Chinese, some of which also come in tea bag form and can be served hot or over ice.

Do I really have to count calories?

If you are obese, you do; if you are overweight, you don't. Do you know how to tell which you are?

3

The Difference Between Overweight and Obesity. How Can I Tell?

What is the difference between overweight and obesity?

Most of my patients use the words "overweight" and "obesity" interchangeably. The two words are not synonymous.

A medical-dictionary definition of obesity describes the condition as "a bodily condition marked by excessive generalized deposition and storage of fat." This means that throughout the body there is an excess of fatty tissue stored beneath the skin. The key word is fat.

Weight, on the other hand, is defined as, "a quantity of heaviness" or "relative heaviness." Overweight, then, may be defined as overheaviness.

What constitutes body weight?

Your body weight is made up of several components, and those such as fat, muscle, and bone, vary for different ages, sexes, and heights. Most people, at one time or another, have consulted a weight chart.

What is the most commonly referred to weight chart?

The one most commonly referred to is issued by the Metropolitan Life Insurance Company. It is based on height, bone structure, and sex, and varies from small frame to large frame

19

for men and women aged twenty-five and over. Desirable weights do not change after the age of twenty-five.

How are weight charts determined? Are they accurate?

The suggested ideal weights are determined from comprehensive studies of the American adult population and are given as the averages for Americans.

There is one factor that is often overlooked. The American population is not a homogeneous one. Not all Americans come from the same ethnic origins, nor do they all live under the same environmental conditions. These are weight factors which will be discussed more fully later on. America's melting-pot tradition makes it unique in the world, for few other countries' populations are made up of so many such diverse cultures. As time passes and the mixing of people and cultures grows, we may one day achieve a truly average-American body build.

Is it true that if you are of the proper weight for your build, height, and sex at the age of twenty-five, that is the weight you should maintain for the remainder of your life?

This is the weight you should strive for throughout your life. These charts are widely used and do not claim to be one hundred per cent accurate, but may serve as a useful guide.

Can I be overweight in terms of my bone structure or muscle development and yet not be obese?

You might be ten to fifteen pounds over the recommended weight of the chart and still not be obese, although you would *look* obese to most people. If so, you would, confusingly, be called non-obese obese. What this means is that to the naked eye, you appear too fat; but actually, your overweight is caused by extra-heavy bone and extremely well-developed muscle. Large-framed and muscularly well-developed professional football players or lady wrestlers fall into this category.

What determines the degree of fatness or obesity?

It is the actual amount of *fat* deposited beneath your skin which determines your degree of fatness or obesity. For this reason, it is possible for you to fit the average of a weight chart and yet be excessively fat—if you have a smaller than average bone and muscle structure. This state is confusingly called obese non-obesity.

What this means is that according to popular standards, you are not overweight; however, if you were to have your body fat-content measured, the results would show the amount of fat underneath the layers of your skin to be proportionately too great to the total amount of bone and muscle.

Can I tell my degree of obesity?

The one foolproof way to determine a person's body-frame or bone structure is by X ray. Usually this is done only for research purposes. A person of small stature is not necessarily small-boned, nor a very tall person necessarily heavy-boned.

The simplest way of measuring the degree of obesity is simply to stand naked in front of a full-length mirror and take a long, hard look. This necessitates complete self-honesty, not always easy for the obese person, as we shall see in a later chapter. But if you can muster the courage to admit to the developing, unwanted rolls of fat in the midsection, thighs, upper arms, etc., you don't need a doctor to tell you you're obese. But you *do* need a doctor to advise you concerning the best and safest way to get down to your ideal weight.

Are there other ways of determining ideal weight?

There are scientific means of determining your ideal

weight, the amount of excess fatty tissue in your body, and
the degree of your overweight or obesity. Many of these
methods can only be used under hospital or laboratory conditions, but there are others which can be employed by the
physician in his own office, with no discomfort to you.

How does my doctor determine my ideal weight?

Physicians often use a simple rule of thumb which gives
them a general idea of the degree of overweight or obesity.
As we have seen, your ideal weight is that weight which you
had attained by the age of twenty-five years; that is, of
course, if you were generally of a fairly lean body build without excess fat. If you are a small woman, five feet tall,
and weighed a desirable 100 pounds at age twenty-five, but at
forty years of age you tip the scale at 125 pounds or more,
you are probably obese. Your bone structure and height have
not changed, and unless you have, during the ensuing fifteen
years, engaged in heavy manual labor, your muscle structure
has probably not changed appreciably. The excess body
weight, however, must have come from somewhere, and that
somewhere was in more fat deposits. A man tends to have
heavier bones and more developed muscle structure, so it
follows that his ideal weight for the same age, height, and
frame will be slightly greater.

How does my doctor tell if I am overweight or obese?

A relatively simple test which your doctor can perform in
his office is the skinfold test. At a point midway between
your shoulder and elbow, measured while your arm is hang-
ing loosely, your physician pinches the skin. He applies a
pair of specially designed calipers and records the measurements in millimeters. According to tables worked out by C. C.
Seltzer and Jean Mayer of Harvard, men having a skinfold
thickness of 23 mm. (approximately one inch) and women
of 30 mm. (approximately 1.2 inches) are definitely obese.
The upper arm is only one place where fat generally does

accumulate, so the skinfold test is taken at various points on your body. In certain kinds of obesity people's arms and legs remain very thin and their weight increase is concentrated in the hips, abdomen, and breasts; but this is the exception, not the rule.

Can I do a simple skinfold test myself?

You can take your own skinfold measurement, and, although it may not be scientifically accurate, you can get a pretty good idea of whether or not you are obese. Take the skin halfway between the shoulder and elbow on the underside of the arm, and with thumb and forefinger pinch it. If you find you have an inch and one-quarter or more of skin between your thumb and finger, then you can be pretty sure your problem is something more than simple overweight.

4

What Theory Fits Your Fat?

Are there sophisticated scientific techniques to determine, to very small fractions, the amount of fat, bone, muscle, and blood in my body?

Yes, for research purposes this can be determined. One of the techniques is the water-submersion method to determine body-fat content. We know that fat tissue is lighter than water; we also know that blood and muscle are slightly heavier, and that bone is much heavier. It is possible to be weighed under water and your specific gravity determined. Specific gravity is the ratio of the weight of the body to an equal volume of water. Since fat tissue weighs less in water than the other components of the body, namely, blood, muscle, and bone, a greater proportion of fat to the rest of the body materials will produce a low specific gravity. Conversely, if you have relatively little fat tissue, the specific gravity will be high—showing leaner body mass or less fatty tissue.

Who conducted this research?

One of the first researchers to use the water-submersion method of determining body-fat content in humans was Dr. Albert Behnke, Jr., a former United States Navy medical officer. In an experiment conducted by Dr. Behnke and W. C. Welham, they measured the specific gravity of seventeen professional football players. To do this, one immerses the person in water and determines the volume of water displaced; obviously, this is not a practical method for the practicing physician, because it must be carried out under laboratory conditions. However, experiments such as these are important, useful, and necessary for accurate scientific research.

What did they find?

Most of us are familiar with the figure of the football tackle over six feet tall, weighing in at some 220 pounds, broad-chested, and usually with large feet and hands. Most of us would guess that this man is certainly overweight, if not actually obese. In fact, all of these men who fall into the large-frame category would fall into the insurance company weight tables as at least ten per cent overweight. Behnke and Welham's findings provide some surprises.

When they measured the specific gravity of the athletes, some of them former All-Americans, they found them to have not only a high specific gravity but an even higher one than is considered normal. That is, the football players had a minimum of fatty tissue. Their better than average weight can be accounted for by their unusual amount of muscle and their heavy bone structure. This situation prevails throughout the athlete's professional life.

What happens when the athlete retires from active sports?

Unless he changes his eating habits, the decrease in activity is bound to affect his weight, as was the case with one thirty-eight-year-old professional athlete.

M. H. had always been heavy but not obese.

During his professional career, this man continuously participated in vigorous physical activities, and in considerably increasing the amount of food he consumed, established heavy eating habits.

Once he retired, his physical activity dropped to a normal level but his eating habits remained the same. The result was a 146-pound gain during his first year of retirement.

Naturally concerned about his excess poundage, he put himself on the so-called "Mayo Clinic Diet" (which the Clinic disclaims completely) and lost eight pounds over a three-month period, but he felt very irritable and very tired.

His excessive fatigue convinced him that he should consult a physician who determined that his basic metabolism rate was minus 25. The doctor diagnosed him as hypothyroid (low thyroid) and gave him thyroid medication. For one month, the patient felt better, but then the feeling of tiredness gradually returned.

After a careful consultation with the patient, who then mentioned his previously self-imposed diet, it was determined that his thyroid function was normal. The drop in his metabolic rate was due to the reducing diet itself. He felt better at first because the thyroid medication had given him a "metabolic kick"; now, however, it was causing his thyroid gland to produce less thyroid hormone itself. This was the cause of his feeling not up to par.

The results of the laboratory tests were explained to the former athlete, and he was taken off the thyroid hormone and put on a special, well-balanced diet. He was also advised to increase his physical activity.

Within three months, he had lost twenty-two pounds and felt like his old self. By the end of two years, the former professional athlete had achieved his ideal weight and has maintained it for three and one-half years.

Two points may be made with this case history. First, when you reduce your level of physical activity you expend less calories, so you must eat less food. When one engages in strenuous physical activity, be it sports or heavy manual labor, he is apt to increase his food intake to provide him with the necessary fuel for the job. Once he stops the heavy work, he'd better count a few calories and say to himself, "Are these mashed potatoes and gravy really necessary?"

Everyone knows what happens when a fireman overstokes a boiler—pressure can build up causing an explosion. When one overstokes the body, there is a kind of "explosion" in weight gain.

A second point is that in determining whether a person is suffering from thyroid deficiency, the evaluation must be made with special care. There is more than one way to test for hypothyroidism, and, in borderline cases, it is advisable to double check and to take into account the patient's history and current daily habits of eating and activity.

Are there other methods to determine body-fat content?

Yes. Another technique is to measure the total amount of potassium in the body. The reason for this is that fat contains practically no potassium, so the relation of the amount of potassium to over-all body size will give an indication of the amount of fat. The greater the amount of fat in the body, the less the proportion of potassium. Conversely, those persons with a greater proportion of lean body mass will have high potassium counts.

I have heard the word "somatotype" used in connection with obesity. Why?

From time to time, medical and other scientific terms once confined to professional conversation creep into the everyday language of the layman. This occurs because of the popular press, newspapers, magazines, radio, and television. For such words one frequently hears in discussions of obesity are: somatotype, endomorph, mesomorph, and ectomorph. Because these words are important in understanding the whole obesity picture and because of the frequency with which one encounters them in the lay press, it might be well to break them down into simple terminology.

Somatotype simply means body type. It comes from the Greek word *soma*, meaning body. The words endomorph, mesomorph, and ectomorph are words describing certain body types or categories.

Do you mean there are actually long, thin types and short, fat types?

As we have already noted, there is more to determining an individual's desired weight than merely noting his age and height. Clearly, body build has to be taken into consideration, for no two persons are exactly alike. For instance, no two five-foot-six people, fifty years of age, and of a roughly determined medium body build are, in fact, exactly the same. Some people are more muscular than others; some are broader through the chests, etc.; and some have proportionately long legs and arms. Others are short-limbed with shorter, rather than longer trunks. Therefore, in accurately determining desired body weight, it is necessary to have a more precise method of determining body types. This effort to type the human body has gone on since early times. Physical Anthropologists C. Wesley Dupertuis and Helen Stimson Dupertuis of the Case Western Reserve School of Medicine in Cleveland, recalling early writings of Hippocrates, point out that the ancient Greek divided people into the two types you mentioned—the long thins and the short fats. Hippocrates also believed that the long thins were prone to lung tuberculosis and that the short fats were more prone to diseases of the cardiovascular system, that is, coronary attack and stroke.

You spoke of endomorphs, mesomorphs, and ectomorphs. What are they?

Although attempts were made through the ages to classify people according to body types, it was not until some thirty years ago, when an American Physical Anthropologist, Dr. William H. Sheldon, published his treatise on somatotyping, or body typing, that we had an acceptable method for describing all the varieties of the human physique.

Sheldon called people who are predominantly round and soft in their bodily appearance endomorphs. In everyday language, such persons are often referred to as "pleasingly plump."

Persons who have hard, angular, and heavily muscled

bodies are called mesomorphs. Generally speaking, persons who perform hard manual labor—as well as professional athletes and others who engage in regular vigorous exercise—develop this body type. The ectomorphs are the slender, delicate types, often tall, but not necessarily so. The high-fashion model fits this category as does the pole-vaulter and the long-distance runner. These persons have few weight problems. Indeed, Jean Mayer, a noted Harvard nutritionist, flatly states, "Girls with long tapering fingers will never get fat."

According to Sheldon's system, every person's body is made up of all three components, but some bodies have one characteristic more prominently in evidence than another, and there are even some who have the three components fairly evenly balanced.

How does body type relate to weight?

According to Dr. Dupertuis, ". . . there is no ideal or normal weight for everyone. There is only a normal weight for the somatotype. It is indeed possible, however, to be under- or overweight for one's own somatotype."

What Dr. Dupertuis is saying is that an insurance-company chart which gives an ideal weight for, let's say, a medium-frame person, obviously has to assume that those medium-frame people are more or less built, if not alike, at least with a great degree of similarity. For example, a person may be of medium bone structure but may be more ectomorph than endomorph or mesomorph in appearance; so his weight, obviously, should not be the same as it is for a person with the same kind of bone but with the broader hips and more fully developed chest and muscles of the mesomorph.

Why don't the insurance companies and other groups who publish ideal-weight tables use somatotype as a basis?

In order to determine "ideals," one must type large segments of the population and then analyze and tabulate the data. To date, this research is still in the early stages, and there are too few physical anthropologists and physicians trained in the fine points of determining somatotypes. However, if and when the knowledge is available, it may help absolve some of the guilt feelings of the definite meso-morphic-endomorph who tries to diet himself into something he isn't and never can be.

There are some people whose body types are obvious. The huge lumberjack, the football halfback, and the heavily built manual laborer are, obviously, heavy framed; however, small persons are more deceptive. One might look at the petite five-foot-two girl with small hands and feet and assume that she is small-boned. She may be; but she may also be medium-boned, or even heavy-boned. This can be determined by X rays of the skull, chest, and long bones.

Has anyone done any scientific research that relates body build to ideal weight?

Yes. Charts were compiled by Dr. and Mrs. C. Wesley Dupertuis from original research by Sheldon (for the men) and data from their own research (for the women).

What are the titles of these charts and how can I read them?

TITLES OF CHARTS:

1. Stature and Average Weight at Age 30 of the 25 Commonest Male Somatotypes Presented in Decreasing Order of Their Incidence in the U. S. Population.
2. Stature and Average Weight at Age 30 of 10 Rare Male Somatotypes from a U. S. Population Presented in Decreasing Order of Rarity.
3. Stature and Average Weight at Age 30 of the 15 Commonest Female Somatotypes Presented in Decreasing Order of Their Incidence in the U. S. Population.
4. Stature and Average Weight at Age 30 of 15 Rare Female Somatotypes in a U. S. Population.

This is how to read the charts: Somatotypes are based on a scale of zero to seven. The first number under somatotype is the endomorph; the middle number, the mesomorph; and the third number, the ectomorph.

For example, if you are a "4 4 3" it means that your endomorphic characteristics are about midway in the scale; in other words, you have a fairly rounded body. The second "4" indicates a moderately muscular body. The "3" indicates that you are slightly ectomorph, meaning you are of average height with medium-length arms, legs, and fingers.

Read these charts only if you have a special interest in somatotyping or if you have been somatotyped and would like to determine your ideal weight.

It must be understood that no one is purely one somatotype. You have at least some element of all three body types. The charts follow.

Chart 1. Stature and Average Weight at Age 30 of the 25 Commonest Male Somatotypes Presented in Decreasing Order of Their Incidence in the U. S. Population

Somatotype	Stature (Inches)	Weight (Pounds)
4 4 3	68.4	160
3 4 4	69.6	152
3 5 3	68.4	158
3 4 3	67.2	143
4 5 2	67.2	169
4 4 4	70.8	169
2 4 4	68.4	135
3 5 4	70.8	167
2 5 3	67.2	140
3 3 5	70.8	146
3 3 4	68.4	138
5 4 2	67.2	176
4 5 3	69.6	177
3 5 2	66.0	149
2 5 4	69.6	150
3 4 5	72.0	160
4 4 2	66.0	151
2 4 5	70.8	144
4 3 4	69.6	153
2 3 5	69.6	133
3 6 2	68.4	156
5 3 3	68.4	166
5 4 3	69.6	186
2 3 6	72.0	140
2 6 3	68.4	156

Chart 2. Stature and Average Weight at Age 30 of 10 Rare Male Somatotypes from a U. S. Population Presented in Decreasing Order of Rarity

Somatotype	Stature (Inches)	Weight (Pounds)
7 1 1	62.4	198
5 1 5	70.8	156
1 1 7	69.6	106
2 1 6	68.4	112
6 1 2	63.6	145
1 7 1	62.4	131
7 1 2	66.0	219
5 1 4	68.4	146
2 1 7	72.0	125
6 1 3	67.2	163

Chart 3. Stature and Average Weight at Age 30 of the 15 Commonest Female Somatotypes Presented in Decreasing Order of Their Incidence in the U. S. Population

Somatotype	Stature (Inches)	Weight (Pounds)
5 3 3	63.3	131
5 3 4	65.6	141
5 3 2	61.1	124
5 2 4	64.4	127
4 3 4	64.4	122
5 4 3	64.4	147
4 3 3	62.2	115
4 2 4	63.3	110
4 2 5	65.6	119
4 3 5	66.7	129
5 3 5	68.9	156
6 3 3	64.4	161
5 2 3	62.2	120
5 2 5	66.7	135
6 3 2	62.2	152

Chart 4. Stature and Average Weight at Age 30
of 15 Rare Female Somatotypes in a U. S. Population

Somatotype	Stature (Inches)	Weight (Pounds)
2 1 6	63.3	89
2 1 7	66.7	99
2 2 5	62.2	91
3 1 5	62.2	93
3 1 7	67.8	110
3 4 2	58.9	100
3 4 4	64.4	120
3 4 5	66.7	128
4 1 4	61.1	95
5 5 3	66.7	174
6 1 3	62.2	129
6 2 5	68.9	169
6 5 2	65.6	204
7 3 4	71.1	278
7 4 3	70.0	301

Do we know what happens to people when they are overfed?
Yes. An enlightening experiment was carried out by Drs.
Sims and Horton of the University of Vermont School of
Medicine. Volunteer prisoners from the State Penitentiary
were deliberately overfed. By having them eat more food
than their body could use, the men—over a period of time—
gained weight. Tests showed the results of this weight gain.

1. Several men more than doubled their body fat, and
   in two of them, the net gain in weight consisted of
   nothing but fat.

2. One-third of the men developed stretch marks in the
   upper thighs and buttocks.

3. After becoming obese, they showed less initiative, were
   less active, and performance in their routine prison as-
   signments lagged.

4. Most of the men developed an aversion to breakfast,
   and a few were not able to keep down the first food
   taken in the morning.

5. Heartburn was common.

6. In spite of the high-calorie diet (up to almost 8,000 calories per day), most of the men developed very real, and, at times, severe hunger toward the end of the day.
7. When the men began the period of weight loss, they found it more emotionally difficult than the enforced weight gain.

Exactly how does this relate to my being fat?

In simple language, Drs. Sims and Horton are saying that the mere fact of becoming obese may produce within your body various chemical changes, including glandular abnormalities and changes in your normal metabolism; but they are careful to say that it is possible for abnormalities in your metabolic process to result in spontaneous obesity, which then produces some of the other body-chemistry changes. The physicians did find that those volunteers who were of leaner body type and had no history of diabetes or obesity lost their forced weight gain with less effort than those whose family history did show these variances.

This research into experimental obesity in man brought to light some other interesting factors which will be discussed in later chapters.

Did this research agree with any other studies?

Sims and Horton's results appear to confirm my research regarding the Yo-Yo Syndrome (see Chapter 6) as well as the research of Dr. Jules Hirsch concerning the number of fat cells we develop in the first few months of life.

Does this mean I am born to be fat or thin?

To some extent this is determined by your fat cells. One of the most recent breakthroughs in the determination of body-fat content has been made by Dr. Jules Hirsch and his associates at Rockefeller University. By using very technical and highly complicated scientific methods, this research team has demonstrated its ability to make an actual count of the number of fat cells in the human body. By taking human fat-cell counts at various stages of growth development, Dr. Hirsch has concluded, from his results, that the actual number of fat cells is determined in the first few months of life. Although our knowledge in this area is in the early stages, it does suggest that early, infant diets might be devised to control the formulation of fat cells. Much more research needs to be completed before we will have the answers, and we must take into consideration hereditary or genetic factors which are very important but whose roles are not entirely determined.

Dr. Jerome L. Knittle, a physician and nutritionist at the National Institutes of Health, has substantiated Dr. Hirsch's work by showing that obese people ". . . have a higher number of fat cells than the non-obese, and the fat cells are generally bigger than in non-obese persons . . ."

If the number of my fat cells is determined long before I can do anything about it, what's the use of trying to lose weight? If I have twice as many fat cells as my thin neighbor, then, of course, I'm going to be fat. Why try?

That sounds reasonable, but that's not the way it works. Drs. Sims and Horton, using the Hirsch method of cell-count and cell-size determination, found that the fat cells of the overfed men increased in size as they gained weight but that the *number* of fat cells remained the same. After the men had reached the excessive weight desired by the researchers, they were gradually reduced to their normal weight, and, with the weight reduction, the fat-cell size gradually decreased, although the initial count remained the same. This is similar to the action of a sponge, which fits my theory.

How does your sponge theory work on me?

The number of fat cells may be determined in early infancy. Just as a sponge with numerous cells will soak up more water and hence become heavier than one with fewer cells, if your number of fat cells is greater than average each of your multitudinous fat cells will absorb fat. You will ultimately increase your weight above the norm. One can squeeze water out of the sponge and even though it then weighs less, the cells remain with the propensity to reabsorb liquid. Similarly, the fat cells in a reduced individual are still there. There is no way in which you can rid your body of them. Unfortunately, they remain present in gross quantities, ready to absorb any ingested fat. The only thing you can do is to avoid an excessive amount of calorie intake throughout your entire lifetime. Exercise will also help.

It will be some time before mother can take Suzie or Johnny to the doctor for a fat-cell count to determine whether or not they will be disposed to obesity in later life. Before such analysis will be of practical application, much more must be learned about hereditary and environmental influences. But this important research breakthrough is one more piece in the difficult jigsaw puzzle of the causes of obesity and the understanding of your complicated physiology.

Are these theories and treatment of obesity known to my doctor?

Probably. Let me speak to your doctor.

5

Doctor to Doctor—For Doctors Only

I learned, as a medical student, that the only way you really gain weight is if you eat more calories than you burn up. Is this still true?

It certainly is true; but you must not stop there, for this is not to say that if you are fat, you must eat like a pig. The real question is: How many calories do you burn? And are you burning an abnormally low number of calories? And, if this is true, what can be done about it in order to help you?

What are the ways of determining how many calories I actually burn?

There are both direct and indirect ways. One such way is to measure the oxygen you breathe in and the amount of carbon dioxide you breathe out. The amount of oxygen can then be converted into the number of calories your body burns. Another is to actually measure the amount of heat your body produces (this is called calorimetry) and thereby measure the energy converted in your body.

Of the food I eat, how much energy goes for heat production and how much energy for useful work?

The majority of your energy goes not for useful work but

for heat production. Approximately seventy-eight per cent goes for heat while only twenty-two per cent goes for your bodily work.

How many fat patients have you actually studied and followed for over five years?

Of the over one thousand patients seen for obesity problems, five hundred have been studied for over five years.

What were the results in these patients?

Forty per cent reached and maintained their ideal weight; thirty-five per cent were continuing to lose weight but at less than optimal weight loss; and twenty-five per cent were "failures."

Why did the twenty-five per cent fail?

They were not sufficiently motivated to follow through on their programs.

Where have these studies been published?

In the following journals:

1. Studying and Treating the Obese Patient, *Maryland State Medical Journal*, 17:64-69, May 1968.

2. The Study and Treatment of the Obese Patient, *Hospital Practice*, 4: 90-94, March 1969.

3. Psychologic Effects of Prolonged Starvation in Extreme Obesity, *Southern Medical Journal*, 63, No. 3:274-279. March 1970.

How do you best treat the obese patient?

There are no clear-cut answers to this question, mainly because obesity is not a disease but a sign of some underlying problem. Whether that problem is psychological or physiological, or both, is of course the determination the physician makes in each case after completion of a careful history, physical examination, and adequate laboratory testing. Only then can specific and appropriate therapy be undertaken.

What is the rationale of your treatment approach?

My treatment approach derives from characteristics of the obese population. This is not a small group in American life; one in five Americans is obese; *i.e.*, more than ten per cent over their ideal weights and accompanied by an excessive amount of body fat. An obese population has an unusual concentration of afflictions; 260 of the original 541 subjects—nearly half—had one or more of the following conditions (the number of patients with each condition is given parenthetically):

Diabetes mellitus (183); arthritis (127); heart disease (87); gout (75); hypertension (61); kidney disease (52); hypercholesterolemia (44); hernia (41); thyroid disease (29); colitis (15); peptic ulcer (7); cancer (3); other conditions (27).

Compared with control subjects, with whom they were matched for age and sex, the obese outpatients had a far greater incidence of metabolic derangements. Those more than fifty per cent obese had a fifty-fifty chance of having an underlying medical abnormality requiring treatment. At thirty per cent obese, the likelihood of having such an abnormality was less, but still significant. Certainly, such data justify a physician's having a strong suspicion of disease in the obese person.

Fewer than ten per cent of the obese outpatients had a bona fide medical abnormality as the original cause of their obesity. But if the metabolic derangements shown were not the initiating cause, they certainly can be regarded as effects of chronic overeating. Notwithstanding the underlying cause of their obesity, the obese population has a higher morbidity rate and, as has been shown innumerable times, a higher mortality rate than the general population. In fact, mortality and morbidity rates increase in direct proportion to the degree of obesity.

You spoke of metabolic derangements found in many of your obese patients. How did these affect their weight problems?

Over fifty per cent of the obese patients showed abnormalities in the way they handled fats, carbohydrates, and/or proteins.

How did obesity affect the patients' behavior?

Behaviorally, the study subjects differed from control subjects of normal weight in significant respects. Of the 541 outpatients, 400 reported that they overate when under stress: facing an examination, losing a job, arguing with relatives, hearing bad news, etc. By contrast, the control subjects and 750 of 1,000 nonobese hospital visitors, and others queried at random, said they tended to undereat when under stress.

Most of the obese outpatients had a history suggesting severely deficient or excessive oral gratification in infancy—either insufficient or excessive nursing at the breast, insufficient or excessive bottle time, or colic. They tended to meet a need for oral gratification by eating (sweets primarily) as well as by smoking cigarettes, pipes, and cigars. That obesity itself may spur this search for oral gratification may be inferred from the preliminary finding that obese persons may have diminished taste-bud discrimination. Apparently, obese persons do not get enough stimulaiton from normal amounts of food.

Does being fat affect one's psycho-physiological performance?

Yes, it has marked effects on an individual's psycho-physiological performance. Twelve obese patients were studied in depth at the Johns Hopkins Hospital, University of Maryland Hospital, and Baltimore City Hospitals. The performance characteristics of a patient who at 350 pounds was one hundred per cent obese are a perfect example of the various decrements found. Compared with the average performance of age-matched men observed in a longitudinal study of aging at the Gerontology Research Center of the National Institute of Child Health and Human Development, located at Baltimore City Hospitals, this individual had the following percentages of normal function: speed of response on simple psychomotor test, forty-four per cent; cardiac output at rest, sixty per cent; maximum ventilation on exercise, twenty-five per cent; maximum breathing capacity, twenty-five per cent; taste-bud discrimination, thirty-three per cent; maximum work rate, fifteen per cent. These results were not calculated as a function of weight.

Does this mean that this man is prematurely aging?
   Yes.

Is there any benefit to be gained from giving this information to the patient?
   Information of this sort is conveyed to patients so that they may appreciate the hazards of obesity. On the positive side, they are told that as weight is reduced and maintained at normal values, morbidity risks also return to normal standards. Functional decrements in the 350-pound man, and in the other eleven in-depth subjects were, in fact, reversed with weight loss. The outpatient studies pointed in the same direction. In addition, after one year of treatment the obese group resembled the healthy control group in selected indicators of metabolic performance. It appears that there are few concomitants of obesity that cannot be reversed in most patients. (One that cannot be reversed seems to be bagginess of the skin; loss of elasticity seems to be a permanent feature of long-term obesity, although exercise affords some improvement.)

You coined the term Yo-Yo Syndrome. What do you mean by it?

Yes, you may be familiar wit what I termed the "Yo-Yo Syndrome," exemplified by the patient who cyclically loses weight and regains all of it—and more. His weight goes up and down repeatedly.

How do you explain this?

A possible explanation is that an important metabolic capacity is weakened or exhausted while the patient is overeating. Then, when he cuts back his caloric intake, his body is unable to metabolize certain foods properly.

The natural history of some hormonal or enzymatic exhaustion in obesity remains to be well documented, but observations in diabetics indicate a possible approach to investigation. In some individuals with a family history or hereditary background of diabetes, sugar intake evokes an increased insulin response until the beta cells of the pancreas can no longer keep pace with the high insulin demand. If the overload persists too long, the insulin-secretion mechanism may be deranged permanently, and/or tissues which are targets of insulin may become less sensitive to it. Our observation of endocrine response in progressive obesity suggests that a similar pattern may prevail in various hormonal systems.

Could enzymes similarly be affected in the obese patient?

Yes. Something akin to this may also happen enzymatically. The output of the enzymes that split fat may decline in response to persistent "overtaxation," and the patient will lay down fat even on a very low-calorie diet. Our laboratory has preliminary data suggesting that twenty per cent of the obese patients studied had reduced blood amounts of enzymes. Lack of enzymes may result in a decreased breakdown of fat.

Which comes first—the hormonal-enzyme problem or the obesity?

At the moment, I do not know whether a particular case of obesity begins with a weakness in the hormonal-enzymatic apparatus or whether obesity induces the weakness. Most probably, in the great majority of cases, obesity occurs because of overeating. Obesity breeds more obesity in a snowball effect as hormonal and enzymatic systems become exhausted in the effort to support the enlarged organism. This hypothesis is currently being tested through our studies aimed at identifying where overloads and failures in the chains of enzymatic and hormonal actions necessary for healthy metabolism are likely to occur. If such information can be obtained, it should permit us to establish profiles of vulnerability to obesity and to pinpoint how obesity snowballs.

Who participated in this study?

Patients from ten to one hundred pounds overweight, although several were more than three hundred pounds overweight. Seventy-three per cent were women and twenty-seven per cent were men. The group included 15 under age 15; 24, age 15 to 20; 271, age 20 to 45; 219, age 46 to 65; and 12 over age 65.

What tests were done?

Laboratory studies—the "maximum" list—were undertaken with this group: a complete study of the blood, including a hemogram; arterial and venous carbon dioxide; thyroxine-by-column; glucose tolerance; serum electrolytes; cholesterol; urea nitrogen; liver function; uric acid; urinary steroids (17-hydroxysteroids and 17-ketosteroids); and qualitative and quantitative amino acid analyses. An electrocardiogram and chest and skull films were also obtained. The skull film was included to check for pituitary lesions such as an eroded sella turcica (found in two patients).

These studies, as well as a comprehensive history of per-

sonal, family, and dietary habits, and a thorough physical
examination, were the basis for the individual regimen.

After the original testing, how often did you see the patients?

As the study continued, appointments were made at
monthly intervals. In these discussions, the patient was informed of the progress or lack of progress he was demon-
strating in terms not only of weight reduction but also
laboratory retesting

Do the patients continue on the same diet?

No, dietary adjustments were made depending on medical
laboratory findings and the patient's reaction to his diet. A
patient who said he had to have a particular food would
be told how to adjust his intake to "make room" for the
otherwise proscribed food. A patient who had to have a
snack after supper was instructed on how to compensate
for this in regular meals.

The patient was told that the name of the game was
"fewer calories in, more calories out." He was encouraged to
exercise. The patient with no weight loss was asked why he
had a problem in adhering to the diet. We conveyed our
concern with disappointments as well as our satisfaction with
progress. The fact that patients were counseled at every appointment by a physician, in addition to other para-medical
workers, may have helped them to appreciate the seriousness
of the weight-reduction attempt.

*Can you suggest any crutches that the patients can use to
help them lose weight?*

I emphasize to patients that anyone who keeps to the diet
must lose weight, barring an undetected abnormality. Some
"crutches" are offered. The patient can obtain oral gratification at low-caloric cost by chewing sugarless gum or drinking
fruit-flavored diet drinks. Motivation is helped by calling the
patient's attention to improvements in his condition. Ideal

weight and ideal measurements become a standard against which the patient can measure his own progress. Changes in physique are reinforcing for both women and men.

Despite counseling and "crutches," some patients could not stay on a diet. Actually, most of the failures dropped out of the study after one or two visits, some voicing resentment that "no magic pill or shot" was offered to do the weight reduction job for them.

Do you suggest that the patient start dieting now or wait?

Tell him to start now, because generally, the greater the amount and duration of obesity, the less likely the chance for success.

What you discuss is fine for a supervised study program, but what can I, as a physician practicing out of my office, do now?

There are a few recommendations I can make, on the basis of our findings, for treating obese patients in your office. The comprehensive history and physical examination, of course, are essential no matter where treatment is given. As a simplified set of screening tests, suitable for treatment in your office, I would suggest these: 1.) thyroxin-by-column to determine the titer of thyroid hormone in the blood; 2.) measurement of two-hour postprandial glucose; 3.) checking venous carbon-dioxide levels for CO_2 retention secondary to extreme hypoventilation; 4.) determination of serum uric-acid levels, because of the propensity toward hyperuricemia in obese patients; 5.) measurement of serum cholesterol and triglycerides because of the high incidence of hyperlipemia associated with obesity; 6.) hematocrit, because of the anemia secondary to fad diets; 7.) complete urine analysis, especially noting any proteinuria or ketonuria; and 8.) testing of respiratory function, which is simply done by asking the patient to pucker his lips and blow out a match burning six inches away.

Combined with findings in your history and physical examination, these laboratory procedures will provide you with a sound basis for prescribing indicated medications, diet, and exercises for most obese patients. The patient should be checked at intervals frequent enough, in your judgment, to maintain motivation, to keep track of medical conditions, and to establish and secondarily reinforce a good nutritional pattern. Where progress is satisfactory, the appointment interval may be lengthened. If, despite good eating discipline, the obesity proves intractable, the patient probably requires study in a hospital or research testing laboratory. A list of these university affiliated Endocrine-Metabolic Departments can be found on pages 216-221.

I am a pediatrician. Does any of your research apply to me?
Yes. An obese baby may become an obese adolescent, an obese adult, and an obese parent whose eating habits are passed on to his children. My study indicates that the desire to eat sweets often stems from an early age when the parent typically offered candy to comfort or bribe a child. You are probably the professional person with the earliest chance of counseling parents against establishing patterns of overeating in their children. By doing so you may help prevent the perpetuation of obesity in the young and in future generations.

Where can I find additional detailed information about the diagnosis and treatment of obesity?
The following are a few of many good articles:

1. Kreisberg, R. A., B. R. Boshell, Di Placido, R. F. Roddam: Insulin Secretion in Obesity. *New England Journal of Medicine,* 176-6, 1967.

2. Bortz, Walter M.: In 500 Pound Weight Loss. *American Journal of Medicine,* 47, #2: 325, 1969.

3. Hirsch, J., J. L. Knittle: Cellularity of Obese and Non-Obese Human Adipose Tissue, *Fed. Proc.*, 1969.

4. Penick, Sydnor B., Albert J. Stunkard: *Medical Clinics of North America*, 54, #3: 745, 1970.

5. Solomon, N., G. J. Dendrinos: Obesity. *Current Diagnosis* 3:657, 1971.

6

The Yo-Yo Syndrome

Who are the Yo-Yos?

For more than ten years, as part of a clinical-research team at Baltimore City Hospitals and the Metabolic Research Ward of Johns Hopkins Hospital, I have been investigating the possibility of physiological causes of overweight. I have been particularly interested in the person who loses, gains, loses and gains again—an all too familiar pattern which I call the Yo-Yo Syndrome.

Following a study of obese patients who were put on a fasting regime of no calories under strict hospital supervision, I began a study of Yo-Yo Syndrome patients on an outpatient basis with a control group of ideal weight patients.

The zero-calorie diet was used solely as a research tool under the strictest medical supervision. This regimen is definitely *not* for home use. Drastic methods, such as total fasting, are unsafe without the closest medical supervision and attention to the health of the patient. Because the patient who is maintained on a starvation diet obviously does not learn the good eating habits necessary to maintain his ideal weight, he only regains the weight on returning to his usual diet. I studied one hundred persons with a previous diagnosis of intractable obesity; obesity which could not previously be reduced. Each of these patients was matched with a control partner of the same age and sex but of normal weight. Eighty-two of the obese and fifty-nine of the normals continued in the study for the full-year period.

What type of abnormalities did the Yo-Yos have?

The results of the study showed that there were aberrations of metabolism among the overweight.

For example, carbohydrate metabolism tests showed thirty-seven per cent of the obese were not metabolizing glucose properly, while only two per cent of the controls showed such an abnormality. Twenty-eight per cent had difficulty with protein metabolism, against two per cent among controls. The difference in fat metabolism was dramatic: seventy-three per cent abnormality among the overweight, with only fourteen per cent among the controls.

Hypothyroidism (defined as an underactive thyroid), which has been the "whipping boy of obesity," was found to be relatively rare, although low basal-metabolic rate was considerably lower than that for the control group. Only nine per cent showed hypothyroidism, against two per cent in controls. Eighteen per cent of the overweight showed abnormal basal metabolism, against two per cent for the controls.

Food intolerance, the inability of some bodies to burn up certain types of food, was found among ninety-six per cent of the overweight, as against thirty-one per cent of the control subjects. Since the initial study of one hundred persons, more than one thousand patients have taken part in the continuing study. The results have led me to believe that *not all*, but *many*, overweight people are metabolically abnormal. I believe that this may be a *result* rather than a *cause* of overweight and that once the deficiency is corrected, diet makes it possible to lose and stabilize weight.

Have you heard of anyone being fat because he had thyroid antibodies?

Yes, I have. The Yo-Yo Syndrome can very often be a clue to the physician that the patient may be a victim of some physiological disorder. Take the case of C. E., a thirty-five-year-old woman who had experienced the Yo-Yo Syndrome over a period of six years.

At the time I examined her, she was twenty-two pounds overweight. Her own physician suspected her to be hypothyroid because of her increased fatigue, increased sensitivity to cold, brittle fingernails, and dry skin. However, her blood tests for thyroid hormone were normal.

Her physician referred her to me for a comprehensive metabolic evaluation, and laboratory tests showed that her blood had an increased amount of thyroid antibodies. When antibodies of a particular substance are present in the blood, they tend to neutralize the normal action of that substance. If one has an abnormal amount of thyroid antibodies, the normal action of the thyroid hormones will be neutralized or rendered ineffective. In order to determine the thyroid antibody count in the blood, fairly sophisticated laboratory procedure is necessary. However, in some instances, the extra expense and work are fully justified.

Once C. E.'s difficulty was properly diagnosed and she was placed on the proper medication and diet, she managed to reach her ideal weight within three months; her antibody problem was stabilized, and her symptoms of hypothyroidism disappeared. She has maintained her weight of 116 pounds for sixteen months.

Can low thyroid be the cause of the Yo-Yo Syndrome?

Yes, it can. Another case of the Yo-Yo Syndrome being a symptom of an underlying physiological problem was the case of P. V.

She was a forty-eight-year-old woman who had had a weight problem most of her adult life. She had been forever gaining and then losing weight; after adhering to a strict diet, she would lose and then gain again. She estimated that over the years she had lost and gained in the neighborhood of four hundred pounds.

She was referred to me and complained of being excessively tired, more forgetful than formerly, and less interested in sex. The interview also revealed that her mother, aunt, and sister had histories of low thyroid function.

Six weeks before her physical examination, she was involved in an automobile accident which resulted in a leg fracture. During her convalescence, she gained forty-three pounds; a further complication was a skin infection under the layers of fat on her breasts and abdomen.

Further examination showed that her body showed abnormal water retention and increased fat storage in the area above her collar bone, waist, and ankles. Laboratory tests proved her deficient in thyroid hormones, showing her to be definitely hypothyroid.

P. V. was placed on a proper thyroid medication and a well-balanced diet, and within eight months she was down to her ideal body weight. In addition, she no longer experienced fatigue, her desire for sex returned, and the skin infections cleared up. For the past three years, she has been able to maintain her desired body weight.

The case of P. V., while not run of the mill, illustrates the necessity for careful and thorough examination and complete laboratory tests, because although the condition of hypothyroidism is found in only a small percentage of obese patients, the possibility cannot be ruled out until the proper tests have been completed and analyzed.

The thyroid gland, as I have noted, has been the "whipping boy" of the overweight society for many generations, despite the fact that increased scientific knowledge has shown that only some eight per cent of obese persons are afflicted with hypothyroidism, or low thyroid function. However, for those persons who do fall into the group of eight per cent, the condition presents a real problem until it is correctly diagnosed and treated.

The case of the person suffering from the Yo-Yo Syndrome is not hopeless. It is important for that person to consult a qualified physician (with some knowledge of endocrinology) who would be willing to take the time to study him thoroughly and do the necessary testing. It is possible that the physician will find the answer, but if the answer is not apparent, the only solution for the Yo-Yo Syndrome victim is to continue dieting until the ideal weight is reached and the body restores itself to normal. Other researchers besides myself, notably Drs. Ethan A. H. Sims and Edward S. Horton at the University of Vermont Medical School, concur in the belief that probably once a person becomes obese, he upsets his own chemistry so that drastic measures must be followed to correct the situation. In other words, obesity apparently tends to perpetuate itself.

Until I go to a doctor can I determine if I am a Yo-Yo?

It is possible for you to learn if you are a victim of the Yo-Yo Syndrome providing you engage in normal everyday physical activity. The following test obviously would not do for a bedridden person or one who leads a more than usually sedentary life. The test is a one-week well-balanced diet of 1,800 calories per day. If you follow it precisely but gain weight at the end of the week, you can be fairly certain that you are in the Yo-Yo Syndrome category.

YO-YO TEST DIET
Meals of 1,800 Calories Per Day
MONDAY

Breakfast

Orange Juice–1 cup
1 Poached Egg
1 Strip Bacon
Whole Wheat Bread–1 Slice
1 pat Butter or Margarine
Coffee with Skim Milk

Lunch

    Broiled Hamburger–Large

    Asparagus–6 Spears

    1 Lg. Baked Potato

    Coffee with Skim Milk or Tea with Lemon

Dinner

    Broiled Lamb Chop–Lean

    Peas & Carrots–¾ cup

    1 Slice White Bread

    Coffee with Skim Milk or Tea with Lemon

    Fruit Cup–½ cup

TUESDAY

    1 Orange–med. size

    1 Soft Cooked Egg

    Whole Wheat Bread–1 Slice

    1 pat Butter

    Coffee with Skim Milk

Lunch

    ⅔ cup Fruit Cup

    1/7 portion of 9″ Apple Pie

    Coffee or Tea with Skim Milk

Dinner

    1 Lg. Slice Lean Roast Beef

    Rice–¾ cup

    Green Beans–1 cup

    Tossed Salad with Lemon Juice

    1 Banana

    Coffee or Tea with Skim Milk

WEDNESDAY

Breakfast
>Grapefruit Juice–¾ cup
>2 Pancakes
>1 tbsp. Syrup
>1 pat Butter
>Coffee with Skim Milk

Lunch
>Tomato Juice–¾ cup
>2 Frankfurters–Boiled
>Cole Slaw–¾ cup
>1 Apricot
>Coffee or Tea with Skim Milk

Dinner
>Clam Chowder–1 cup
>1 Lg. Veal Chop, Broiled
>Mashed Potatoes–1 cup
>Salad Greens
>Angel Cake–Small Wedge
>Coffee or Tea with Skim Milk

THURSDAY

Breakfast
>½ Grapefruit & 1 tsp. Sugar
>Omelet of 1 Egg & 1 pat Butter
>Whole Wheat Bread–1 Slice
>Coffee with Skim Milk

Lunch
>Sandwich: Turkey or Peanut Butter
>Lettuce & Tomato
>Coffee with Milk or Tea with Lemon

Dinner

    Boneless Lean Ham, Broiled–Large Slice
    1 cup Noodles, 1 pat Butter & 1 tbsp. Grated Cheese
    Cabbage–½ cup
    Tomato Salad
    1 Apricot
    Coffee with Skim Milk or Tea with Lemon

FRIDAY

Breakfast

    ½ Grapefruit, 1 tsp. Sugar
    Corn Flakes–1 cup, with Skim Milk–8 o.z
    1 tsp. Sugar
    Coffee or Tea with Milk

Lunch

    Clear Soup–1 cup
    Salmon Salad Plate with little Mayonnaise, Lettuce &
       1 Tomato
    1 med. Plain Roll
    ½ cup Canned Fruit Cocktail, no Syrup
    Coffee or Tea with Skim Milk

Dinner

    ½ Avocado Pear
    Scallops–Broiled–1 cup
    1 Med. Baked Potato
    1 cup Cooked Beets
    1 Slice White Bread
    Coffee with Skim Milk or Tea with Lemon

SATURDAY

Breakfast
   1 med. Orange
   2 Pancakes (about 4″ diameter)
   1 pat Butter
   1 tbsp. Syrup
   Coffee with Skim Milk

Lunch
   Chicken Salad Sandwich or Ham & Lettuce on White
      (very little Mayonnaise)
   Coffee with Skim Milk or Tea with Lemon

Dinner
   Meat Loaf–Large Slice
   Mashed Potatoes, 1 cup
   1 cup Snap Beans
   1 pat Butter
   Tossed Lettuce with Lemon Dressing

SUNDAY

Brunch
   Orange Juice–1 cup
   2 Poached Eggs and 2 strips Bacon–5″
   Coffee Cake, 1 avg. size serving
   Coffee with Skim Milk

Dinner
   Steak–Broiled–med.
   French Fried Potatoes–8 sticks
   Mixed Green Salad with little Dressing
   Beer–12 oz. glass
   1 Apple or Banana
   Coffee with Skim Milk or Tea with Skim Milk

After dieting and losing weight, if I overeat a bit I gain an inordinate amount of weight. Why?

The reason, most probably, is that you eat food containing an excessive amount of salt. This salt causes you to retain an inordinate amount of fluid and thus causes the excessive weight gain.

Why do I always have the greatest weight loss at the beginning, regardless of what diet I start on?

The main reason for the quick weight loss is because you are ridding your body of its excess fluid.

7

Why Do You Overeat?

What makes you want to eat? Why do you sometimes eat more than at other times? What makes you begin to eat? And what makes you stop?

We know that when we walk, sit, or lie down, there is a mechanism in the brain which tells the body to do these things and tells the body which muscles to use. We think there are similar centers in the human brain by which food intake is regulated.

Just what part of my brain helps me decide how much food to eat before it signals "enough"?

Considerable research is being carried out to better understand tne mechanisms which regulate the amount of food you eat and why you get hungry. The brain, as we know, is made up of various parts, all having specific functions. Deep in the center of the brain is a group of nuclei known as the hypothalamus. It is called the hypothalamus because it is beneath, or under, another part of the brain, the thalamus. The word is taken from the Greek *hypo*, meaning below or beneath, and *thalamus*, meaning a chamber. Both the thalamus and the hypothalamus are sections of another part of the brain called the diencephalon, derived from two more

Greek words; *dia,* meaning through, and *encephalon,* meaning brain.

It is important to understand this part of brain anatomy because it is precisely these parts of the brain which are believed to be the food-regulating and satiety centers of man and other vertebrate animals.

How was this discovered?

The first clue to the importance of the hypothalamus in the study of obesity and hunger came when it was discovered that animals who had sustained lesions or injuries to the front-center section of the hypothalamus became obese. It was also learned that when each of the sides of the hypothalamus are destroyed, the result is a cessation of eating and drinking.

Researchers, including Dr. Jean Mayer and his colleagues at Harvard University, where extensive research into the function of this tiny gland has been going on for years, have been able to produce obesity in animals by surgically producing a lesion in the hypothalamus.

Does this ever happen in humans?

Yes; this discovery led to the further discovery that, in rare instances, obesity in humans is possibly due to a lesion of the hypothalamus. The causes of the lesion may vary, but the result is a voracious appetite—with no apparent control —which results in obesity.

Have you ever seen a patient like this?

Yes, such was the case of A. A., a youth of twenty-one. The patient had never experienced a weight problem prior to his excessive weight gain of twenty-one pounds; however, six months prior he had had epidemic encephalitis, commonly called sleeping sickness.

The illness had produced a lesion of the hypothalamus. In addition to the steady, rapid weight gain, A. A. complained of excessive fatigue, severe headaches, was over-irritable, and experienced severe convulsions.

Laboratory tests and data on brain waves confirmed an earlier diagnosis of brain damage caused by the encephalitis.

A. A. was treated with anti-convulsant medication and placed on a special diet. Within two months, his symptoms had subsided, and within four months, his weight had returned to normal. He has been able to maintain his weight for three and one-half years and has been without a convulsion.

Why do I still feel hungry after a meal that satisfies another?

Research in this area is still in its relative infancy, and there is disagreement among researchers as to the exact location of all the control centers, and just how important are the functions of those whose activity we can isolate. In short, medical science is working on the problem, mostly with experimentation on animals, such as rats, mice, dogs, cats, and monkeys. Some day we probably will be much better able to understand the functions of various mechanisms in the human brain and, in turn, of those which influence the amount of food we eat and those which give us a feeling of being "full."

How does metabolism, the way I burn up my food, affect my weight?

Metabolism, low and high, has been blamed for more fat and thin people than is actually the case. Your metabolic rate is the speed with which your body causes normal chemical changes to take place, thus causing energy transformations. It is what determines how efficiently you use your own body fuel. An abnormally low metabolic rate means that one or another of your five successive stages of nutrition may not be occurring at a desired rate.

You take into your body foodstuffs which consist of carbohydrates, fat, and protein. These foodstuffs are then broken into building blocks, absorbed into the blood stream, and used by the body. Some of the by-products of the foodstuffs that are absorbed into the body are used for energy. This means that these substances are broken down, with the release of energy, into carbon dioxide and water. This energy can then be used for all your body functions, and to keep you alive. Without this energy, you would be dead; however, it is not true that all chemical reactions release energy; some actually need energy.

A high metabolism produces an excess of energy, and the person's food intake cannot keep up with his energy requirements. This person obviously will have no overweight problem, but it must be emphasized that neither too low nor too high metabolisms are desirable. Temperature also modifies metabolism. An increased temperature increases metabolism and decreased temperature decreases it. The ideal body, of course, is the one which uses its fuel most efficiently, just as a highly prized automobile is one which gives the best performance for its fuel consumption.

Is it possible that even though I limit my calories, there are some foods that I cannot eat without gaining weight?

Yes. This assertion by laymen has generally been pooh-poohed in the past; but today, medical science has shown that in some instances, you may be absolutely right. In cases of maturity-onset diabetes, for example, your body does not metabolize carbohydrates properly. In these cases, the body is less sensitive to the action of insulin. In other words, there is usually plenty of insulin present in the blood, but for some yet unknown reason, it does not act optimally upon carbohydrates. For this reason, the maturity-onset diabetic must not eat more carbohydrates than his body can tolerate.

Are there other ways metabolism can affect weight?

Yes. Some people are victims of faulty protein metabolism and still others have trouble metabolizing fat.

A twenty-eight-year-old woman, G. N., was forty-two pounds overweight and had a history of continual ups and downs in her weight. Before her referral, she had, unfortunately, consulted a "weight-reduction mill" and immediately, without proper examination, was started on a daily dose of three grains of desiccated thyroid; eventually, the dose was increased until she was taking fifteen grains daily. She began to have some alarming symptoms; throbbing headaches, excessive sweats, diarrhea, and increased irritability. She was clearly showing the symptoms of an overdose of thyroid hormones.

At this point, her family doctor, who found out about the situation, was alarmed, and asked that I study her. I immediately took her off the thyroid medication. Her medical history also revealed that she had not had a menstrual period for the past four years. After being taken off the thyroid medication, she continued to experience lack of menstrual periods and her basal-metabolic rate was very low. An important point is that obesity *alone*, when it is not associated with low-thyroid hormone, can cause a low basal-metabolism rate. The prescription for this condition is not thyroid medication but weight reduction *only*. Her blood tests for thyroid hormone were normal, but they did show an increased amount of fatty substances in the blood.

The patient was then placed on medication to decrease the amount of fatty substances in her blood, and was also placed on a low-calorie, low-fat diet. Her tests had shown that her body had difficulty metabolizing fats. She was not given any thyroid medication. After ten months of treatment, her symptoms subsided, her menstrual periods returned to normal, and she achieved her ideal weight. The fatty substances in her blood decreased to normal amounts.

This young woman has maintained her ideal weight, without medication, for the past six years.

Do you see other odd, unexplainable conditions that may hinder weight loss?

Once in a great while. G. M., a thirty-nine-year-old woman, had experienced the Yo-Yo Syndrome for three years and was twenty pounds overweight at the time she was examined by me. Her weight fluctuations were so great and so unusual that she was finally hospitalized for more careful observation. During this time, it was noted that her weight changed from three to seven pounds per day depending upon the amount of salt eaten and the amount of fluids drunk. Her discomfort was aggravated by swelling of her legs and feet.

It is not unusual to find a weight gain in fluids proportionate to the amount of salt in the diet; however, the interesting and unusual thing about this patient was that her body fluid also fluctuated with changes in atmospheric temperature and humidity.

This was ascertained by placing the patient in an air-conditioned room, where temperature and humidity were controlled. When the temperature and humidity remained constant, her usual daily weight changes subsided, but when the air conditioning was turned off, she immediately began to retain more fluid.

Once the cause of her condition was determined, she was released from the hospital, instructed to stay in an air-conditioned room as much as possible, and was placed on a low-salt, special diet. She was also given medication to relieve the excessive fluctuations of the swelling in her feet and legs.

Within two months, the extreme weight swings had diminished and the patient had lost the twenty pounds of excess weight. She has been able to maintain her ideal weight for two years and has not been bothered by the wide fluctuations of weight due to fluid retention.

What takes place in the body when you eat and drink?

1. Chewing and swallowing—you take food into your mouth, grind it up, and swallow.
2. Digestion—you break down food into small components.
3. Absorption—you take these small components from the gastrointestinal tract into your blood stream.
4. Assimilation—you reassemble these small components in the liver, and use them as building blocks.
5. Excretion—you get rid of waste materials, by breathing, perspiring, urinating, or defecating.

Is this nutrition?

This process is our first definition of nutrition: tissues are built up and energy freed.

What is the second description of nutrition?

This pertains to "the study of the food-and-drink requirements of human beings for growth, activity, reproduction, and production of milk." In other words, what happens when the nutrition process is effective.

What else determines the amount of food we eat?

Not all weight problems, whether having to do with too little or too much weight, are the result of metabolic malfunction; it is only one of the factors that determine our food intake. The regulating mechanism in the brain is another. Dehydration, psychological factors, and external stimuli also affect the amount of food we eat.

What makes us want to eat?

Food can be, and frequently is used as, a kind of tranquilizer, pacifier, and substitute for love and attention. Marital problems, whether real or imagined, often provide the impetus to seek solace in food. Both men and women are subject to this problem, but the incidence is higher among women, particularly nonworking wives, because they are at home, in close proximity to the refrigerator. More often than not, the food is also a substitute for the sexual satisfaction they no longer experience.

Mrs. R. L. was thirty-two years old when she was referred for help. Although she always had a tendency to gain weight and had to be careful of her eating habits, she had possessed a beautiful figure admired by husband and friends alike.

Substituting food for sex, she, in fact, became a *"foodaholic"* and actually believed that she had become addicted to food. In order to escape having sexual relations with a husband who she believed did not love her, she kept eating indiscriminately.

The result of this somewhat irrational behavior was that she received more and more attention; her weight was a constant topic of her husband's conversation. She also received more attention from her children, who wanted to prevent their mother from gaining additional weight and showed their concern by repeatedly telling her not to eat fattening food. The result of this new and welcome attention had a snowballing effect. Her fatness was related to decreased sexual satisfaction which resulted in her eating more, becoming fatter, and having less sex. She avoided social functions and blamed it on her fatness. Instead of doing things, she found herself daydreaming about doing them. The habitual daydreaming and lack of activity decreased her energy expenditure which further contributed to the weight gain.

When she was examined by me, I found that in addition to her thirty-one pounds of excess weight, she was deficient in thyroxin, the active iodine compound existing normally in the thyroid gland. Within four months of being placed on the proper medication and a special, well-balanced diet which she, fortunately, adhered to, she lost the excess weight.

Her sex drive returned, and she was able to resume her relationship with her husband. For the past six years, she has maintained her ideal weight.

Is there a difference between appetite and hunger?

Latest statistics show that some twenty-five million persons in the United States suffer from hunger. We do not say that these hungry people suffer from lack of appetite.

What role does my appetite play?

Most mothers brag about their children's hearty *appetite* or bemoan the lack of *appetite* in little Johnny. Nurses and physicians take a "good appetite" as an encouraging sign during illness or convalescence.

Appetite is a complex of sensations which makes one look forward with a degree of pleasure to eating. These sensations may be created by delectable odors emanating from the kitchen, or a good brisk walk before a meal which the eater knows will contain one or more of his favorite foods. Each of these elements, or a combination of them, leads one to exhibit what I normally refer to as an appetite. In the case of a convalescent patient, certain medications are sometimes given to "increase the appetite," that is, to increase the desire to eat. In other words, we think of appetite in a pleasurable way.

I understand about appetite, but, then, what is hunger?

Hunger, on the other hand, does not conjure up a pleasant image. If you have ever been truly hungry, you know full well that it is unpleasant. A short delay in the usual mealtime may increase the appetite, but prolonged delay will begin to produce the unpleasant symptoms of hunger. The physical sensations of hunger increase irritability, as any dieter who has tried "crash dieting" well knows. Actual physical pain in the stomach region is common, and energy decreases.

What will prolonged hunger do to me?

Prolonged hunger is a very unpleasant sensation; carried to extremes, hunger has been known to make men steal, kill, or even resort to cannibalism. Anyone who has fasted for any length of time knows that the gnawing hunger pains seem to go away after the third day. The answer to this seeming paradox is that the body has re-regulated itself and is, in fact, being fed. The more active the fasting person is, the faster the body's food reserves are used up. As these reserves are used up, we come closer and closer to the state of starvation.

What will starvation do to me?

Even a relatively short period of starvation, without medical supervision, can lead to harm to your body. Prolonged starvation ultimately leads to death.

Have there ever been any experiments done on what influences hunger and appetite?

Yes; Dr. Stanley Schachter, a social psychologist at Columbia University, has done some interesting experiments concerning those influences which affect hunger, appetite, and the amount of food we eat. His investigations were prompted by the work of Drs. T. B. Van Itallie and S. A. Hashim of St. Luke's Hospital, New York City.

At St. Luke's, a group of obese volunteers, with another two persons of normal weight as controls, were selected as inpatients so that their food intake could be studied. A measured-calorie, liquid diet was devised; one which was palatable but extremely dull and uninteresting. Each patient, after being thoroughly examined medically with case histories—including eating patterns—duly recorded, was assigned a hospital room where there was a "feeding machine." The obese patient was told that whenever he was hungry all he had to do was press the lever and the liquid diet would be dispensed through a tube. He was also told that he could eat as much as he wished. What the patient did not know was that each time he took a sip of the calorie-measured liquid, the amount was duly recorded on a graph. The liquid formula contained fifty per cent carbohydrate, twenty per cent protein, and thirty per cent fat. Vitamins and minerals were also added in amounts adequate for daily maintenance.

All that the patients had to do was put the tube in their mouths and a measured amount of formula would be released. Several interesting things happened.

The two normal-weight individuals maintained their normal weight. One of the normal subjects was allowed to eat at will, but he voluntarily maintained a three-meal-a-day pattern. The second normal-weight man was given the machine only at those times corresponding to breakfast, lunch, and dinner. All the obese subjects were allowed to eat at will.

The eating patterns of the obese subjects were markedly different. One four-hundred-pound, twenty-seven-year-old man consumed only 275 calories (plus or minus fifty-seven) a day when using the feeding machine. He was, obviously, not eating enough to maintain his four-hundred-pound weight. In order to see whether the feeding machine itself was inhibiting the man's eating, after eighteen days he was given a pitcher of formula and a cup and, again, allowed to drink as much as he liked, whenever he chose. His caloric intake increased to about five hundred calories daily. After twenty-six days with the pitcher-and-cup routine, he was returned to the feeding machine, and immediately the amount he drank decreased.

Following the experiment, the subject went home where he followed a diet regimen of four hundred calories daily. He reported to the clinic weekly, and at the end of 252 days, he weighed in at two hundred pounds. Sad to report, within a couple of years he had gained back all the lost weight—he just couldn't diet.

A thirty-six-year-old woman, weighing 390 pounds, followed about the same pattern, although her caloric intake during the feeding-machine period was even lower than her male counterpart's. She drank only 144 to 235 calories a day.

When given the cup and pitcher, she upped her caloric count to between 442 and 632 calories. Three more obese subjects followed a similar eating pattern, with the feeding machine apparently an inhibiting factor.

Why did the normal-weight persons eat just enough to maintain their weight and why did the obese patients eat much less than enough to maintain their weight; in fact, so little, that they lost large amounts of weight?

There are several factors which may have influenced the obese subjects' eating patterns. First of all, they were all grossly obese, and obviously volunteered because they hoped to lose weight. There is the first factor, motivation. Drs. Van Itallie and Hashim also reasoned that eating through a tube is pretty rudimentary and dull, therefore cutting down the pleasure usually associated with eating. The cup-and-pitcher experiment only slightly increased the amount of formula consumed. It is possible that the increase was due to the more acceptable way of consuming food, but the monotony of the food may have been another deterrent to consuming more formula.

Drs. Van Itallie and Hashim say: "Whether the inhibition of food intake exhibited by obese patients represents a physiologic effect of massive stores of fat, or whether it results from psychologic factors relating to guilt about the obesity, fear of the feeding device, inability to adjust to the formula, or some other cause, is unknown . . ."

The experiments at St. Luke's Hospital led Dr. Schachter and Columbia University associates Ronald Goldman and Melvyn Jaffa, to conduct some interesting studies. He surmised that perhaps there were external stimuli which contributed to the eating behavior of obese persons, and he set up the following experiment.

Dr. Schachter believes that "the set of physiological symptoms considered characteristic of food deprivation are not labeled as hunger by the overweight. In other words, *the overweight person literally may not know when he is physio-*

logically hungry. This may seem to be a remote possibility, but it appears to be the case."

Under the guise of a taste test, Dr. Schachter and his associates conducted an experiment to try out his theory about hunger responses. For his subjects he used two groups of male undergraduates at Columbia College; each student was tested individually.

One group of students was asked not to eat the meal preceding the experiment, either lunch or, in this case, dinner. They were told that the fasting was necessary to prevent their taste discrimination from being impaired.

Then, since the object was to fill the stomachs of one group and keep the other group with empty stomachs, the first group, containing both normal-weight and overweight men, were left in a room where there was a stack of roast-beef sandwiches on the table. They were all told to eat as many as they wanted until they were satisfied. They ate for fifteen minutes and at the same time filled out a food-preference questionnaire.

The empty-stomach group was seated in front of five bowls of crackers and asked to taste the different kinds of crackers and given a taste sheet to note how the crackers tasted; salty, cheesy, garlicky, etc.

Before they were allowed to eat the crackers, some were told they were to be subjected to nonpainful electric stimulation so that the researchers could study the effect of tactile stimulation on taste. This fiction was invented to produce what Dr. Schachter calls Low Fear. In order to stimulate High Fear, part of the group were shown a phony electric-shock machine and told the same story, only with the added warning that the shocks would be painful. Then the students, the Full Stomachs and the Empty Stomachs, began to eat, taste, and rate the crackers for the next fifteen minutes.

Here was a group of people overweight and normal, empty and full, frightened and calm. In this way, Dr. Schachter was able to study the eating behavior of the subjects under the guise that they were participating in a taste test.

As expected, the normals ate fewer crackers when their stomachs were full. But, and here's the surprise, the fats ate as much or slightly more when their stomachs were full as when they were empty. Dr. Schachter concludes that the actual state of the stomach has nothing to do with the eating behavior of the overweight.

Dr. Schachter also found that the High Fear normals ate considerably fewer crackers, but that fear had little or no effect on the overweight. In fact, the High Fear overweight people ate slightly more than the calm fatties. This led the psychologists to conclude that the overweight do not label as "hunger" the same set of bodily symptoms that normals recognize.

Following this line of reasoning, Dr Schachter suggests that there is a distinction between external and internal control of eating behavior. He says: "Presumably, eating behavior is a joint function of the purely internal or physiological cues we commonly associate with the state of food deprivation and of largely external cues such as smell, taste, the sight of other people eating, etc., all food-related cues independent of the purely visceral correlates of the hunger state. Obviously such cues affect everyone's eating behavior."

This leads to the theory that the eating behavior of the overweight is, in very large part, under external control and relatively unrelated to the state of the stomach. On the other hand, the eating behavior of a normal person is regulated by *both* external and internal cues.

In another, quite different experiment where wall clocks were manipulated to run either fast or slow so that the subjects thought it was either past dinner time or too early for dinner, the results were fascinating. In the overweight group, the fast-time subjects ate almost twice as much as those on slower time. This indicates that the mere suggestion

that it is time for dinner is a spur to eating for the overweight. On the other hand, the slow-time normals were inclined to refuse to eat in order not to spoil their dinner. It
appears that eating crackers or anything else does not spoil
dinner for the fat subject.

If one's wish to eat is triggered by stomach contractions
and the smell of dinner cooking, then it is reasonable to
expect that there is some kind of stop mechanism that says,
"enough!" In normals, this mechanism is obviously in working order, but with the obese it appears to fail to signal
satisfaction. In fact, Dr. Schachter has shown in experiments
that fat people "eat just as much in an experimental eating
situation conducted immediately after they have eaten a
meal as they do when they have been deprived of food for
some ten hours, whereas normal subjects, of course, eat considerably more after food deprivation than they do when they
have eaten a meal."

Dr. Schachter openly admits that there is a multiplicity
of elements which contribute to overweight in any one person; however, he believes that the evidence shows that the
case for external stimuli as a salient factor in the study of
the problem is extremely important.

In another experiment during Yom Kippur, the Jewish Day
of Atonement and the most sacred of Jewish Holy Days,
total fasting for a twenty-four-hour period is commanded by
Biblical Law. The orthodox Jew must go without food or
water for this period, beginning on Yom Kippur Eve. Except
to go home to sleep, he virtually spends the entire twenty-
four hours in prayer at his synagogue.

Dr. Schachter and his team sent out questionnaires to 456
Jewish men and women. Of these, 296 persons replied—160
men and 136 women. 212 said that they attempted fasting.
Of these fasters, 49 Jews were classified as obese, whereas
the remaining ten obese Jews did not fast. In other words,
83.1 percent of obese Jews fasted as contrasted with 163

out of 237 among the normal-weight subjects. This represents 68.8 percent, or almost fifteen per cent fewer.

Included in the questionnaires were questions related to the degree of unpleasantness the subject felt during the fast. The criteria ranged from extremely unpleasant to not at all unpleasant. As expected, the obese Jews found the fast correspondingly less unpleasant than their thinner counterparts.

The Goldman, Jaffa, and Schachter data suggest that when the obese person is removed from an environment that possesses external stimuli to eating, such as the odor of cooking food, television food commercials, and odors from commercial bakeries and restaurants on the street, he is less inclined to crave food. This supports the theory that at least in the case of numerous obese persons external factors play an important part in how much they eat and, more importantly, when.

For the non-obese faster, the sensation is fairly unpleasant, and it appears that it matters little whether he is in a controlled environment or his normal one. It seems that the normal-weight individual's food-regulating mechanisms are operating normally, while perhaps the obese's are not. There is still much to learn before scientists will be able to draw definite conclusions. We must learn more about the food-regulating mechanisms and how and why they work or don't work, we must know about hereditary influences, and we must study more closely the environmental factors surrounding the obese patient.

The Columbia study is interesting and helpful, but, clearly, we must make similar studies under more closely controlled situations and with larger groups of subjects before definite conclusions can be drawn. For more scientific accuracy, such studies would be of more value if complete medical data on the subjects were included, to rule out possible physiological aberrations.

8

You Really Are What You Eat

What has brought about the interest in nutrition today?

The upsurge in the interest in nutrition—the greatest since the discovery of the importance of vitamins—was sparked by the discovery that some twenty-five million Americans not only go to bed hungry but that the *quality* of their food, as well as the quantity, is unsatisfactory. This revelation prompted Dr. Jean Mayer, White House Consultant on Nutrition, to call the first White House Conference on Nutrition in 1969. Nutritionists also point out that many of our more affluent citizens are also poorly nourished, even the overweight!

If this is indeed true, what can be done to prevent it in the future and how can the situation as it is today be improved?

Nutrition is a lot more than counting calories, weighing food, and making up menus to fit a particular person's needs. It is an integral part of the study of man, for if we want to know what makes man tick, we must know what his fuel requirements are, just as we must know the fuel requirements for inanimate machines. We must also learn to recognize that when these fuels are not taken in the correct proportions, the human machine does not operate at maximum

74

capacity. Knowledge of nutrition is not pulled out of the air, nor dependent on far-out theories, but is grounded on the basic sciences, with special emphasis on chemistry, biochemistry, and physiology. Chemistry and biochemistry are two of the most important sciences in the study-and-research programs in nutrition experimentation.

This sounds very technical. What portion of this knowledge of nutrition will help me now?

Broadly speaking, in this book we are concerned with three aspects of nutrition: good nutrition, or the well-balanced diet; over-nutrition and under-nutrition; and the results of each. We are concerned not only with the quantity of food, which may be excessive in the overweight person, but the quality of that food.

What is a well-balanced diet?

A term familiar to all of you is "balanced diet." When your doctor tells you, when dieting, to maintain a balanced diet he probably means one that has adequate amounts of carbohydrate, fat, protein, vitamins, and minerals.

I am interested in the quality of different kinds of food and their value to your body through a well-balanced diet which, for most humans, can be met by daily eating a combination of foods from four broad categories: the milk group; meat group; vegetables and fruits; and breads and cereals.

The milk group includes not only milk but also cheese, ice cream, and other foods made with milk. Included in the meat group are fish and poultry and, for vegetarians, dry beans, peas, and nuts as alternate foods; this does not mean that non-vegetarians cannot on occasion substitute these foods for meat.

Fruits and vegetables are fairly self-explanatory, but it must be emphasized that variety is important; green leafy vegetables are important, as are yellow vegetables, such as squash and carrots. Similarly, you should not confine your

fruit diet to apples and pears, for you also need the citrus
fruits, such as oranges and grapefruit.

Whole-grain and enriched cereals and bread supply you
with valuable amounts of needed essentials.

The exact amount of each of these foods you need is for
your physician to decide. Nutritional needs are individual,
for as I have already stated, no two body chemistries are
the same; it is only logical that, as the chemical mechanism
varies, its fuel requirements will also vary. For some of you,
health problems such as diabetes or high-cholesterol counts
will dictate the elimination of some foods and the substitution
of others, but again, these decisions must be made under
medical supervision.

What, basically, makes up my body?

We know that the body is a complex mechanism made up
of millions and millions of cells and that these cells are of
many kinds, shapes, and sizes. Each of these cells, in order
to live, must have the proper nourishment, and for each kind
of cell, there are specific food requirements. Knowledge in
this field is still not complete, but we are learning more each
day, particularly as our research in biochemistry progresses.

*Since there are different requirements for different cells, is
there such a thing as perfect balanced nutrition?*

Dr. Roger J. Williams, a noted biochemist and the dis-
coverer of pantothenic acid, a part of the Vitamin B_2 complex, which is a diet essential, says in his book, *Nutrition in
a Nutshell:* "Perfect cellular nutrition throughout our whole
bodies, in the sense that every cell gets exactly what it
needs for maximum efficiency, is probably as rare as perfect
health or as perfect human conduct. To err is human, but
this does not make it desirable to make as many errors as
possible."

How is cellular nutrition determined?

This is determined in the laboratory by taking a sample of the particular tissue, studying the cells, and analyzing them to determine their composition. Each cell lives in its own fluid which surrounds and nourishes it. When we take a culture or a sample of a tissue containing one kind of cell, we must grow it in a solution. Depending on the composition of the solution, the cell will flourish, show retarded growth, or die. It is possible to study cell-growth and development in the laboratory and then transfer this knowledge to human needs.

It would hardly be feasible intentionally to deprive humans of essential nutrients to see if their bones would deteriorate or their brain cells atrophy. However, it is possible to take the knowledge we have acquired under the microscope and in the test tube and apply it to experimental animals other than humans. It is certainly true that what happens inside a rat is not necessarily the case with a human, but experimentation with rats can, and often does, provide clues to our own nutritional needs. Rats are not the only animals used in medical research. Primates, such as chimpanzees and gorillas, are more closely akin physiologically to humans, but they are not practical for large-scale investigation because of the cost and scarcity of the animals.

If I am healthy will my cells be healthy, and vice versa?

Yes. It cannot be too strongly emphasized that the human body (like all animals and even plants) is made up of a complex system of living cells and therefore must eat to live (not live to eat). How healthy they remain is in direct proportion to the health of the individual. Within your body, there is an interdependence among the cells. Some cells act as auxiliaries in that they, in themselves, are not vital to life but they provide the passage so that nourishment can get through to vital, life-sustaining cells.

We have seen dramatic evidence of this in the case of a

forty-four-year-old man, R. B. In this instance, reckless dieting, resulting in poor nutrition, led to a "chain reaction"
which ultimately affected his heart cells.

He had been overweight since the age of thirty-six and
had suffered from the Yo-Yo Syndrome for the past eight
years. During this eight-year period, he lost and gained over
two hundred pounds. He finally became frustrated and dis-
gusted with his failure to maintain his weight loss and for
that reason went on a daily regimen of eight glasses of
water and all the lettuce he could eat.

During the first week of this crash diet, he lost fifteen
pounds, and lost six more during the second week. On the
fifteenth day, he collapsed, was rushed to the hospital, and
was admitted in shock. Laboratory tests showed that his
potassium reserves were very low and that he was losing
nitrogen. Actually, his body tissues were being broken down
and converted to sugar.

A thorough physical examination revealed that he had,
in fact, suffered a mild coronary heart attack. His potassium
was replaced through medication. He was placed on a well-
balanced diet during his twenty-one-day stay in the hospital
and after his recovery. He lost weight at the rate of one
pound a week until he had lost fourteen pounds. He has
maintained a stable weight for the past five years.

The case of R. B. is an extreme example of the serious
metabolic trouble which may be caused by a person going
on his own diet. The eight glasses of water per day caused
him to lose not only water, but potassium. (The potassium
loss came about through excessive urination.) His lettuce
diet did not enable him adequately to replace the potassium,
so the resulting potassium deficiency caused him to go into
shock because of the severe effect on the heart. This resulted
in lowering his blood pressure so much that he was not
pumping enough blood to reach his heart or to supply the
heart muscle. In addition, his diet did not have the necessary vitamins, minerals, and protein, so that he went into

negative nitrogen balance. R. B.'s body tissues, including heart tissue, were being broken down and converted to sugar to supply his body with energy. This further complicated his heart problem.

Obviously, no competent physician would allow a patient to indulge in such an improper diet. This is a good example of the results of dieting without medical supervision and indicates how the interdependence of body cells can chain react to cause trouble.

Why was nutrition so important to the heart cells?

Another interdependent relationship is between the cells of the heart and its arteries. Everyone knows that when the heart stops beating, we die. The heart is a pump which sends blood continuously throughout the body, and even to the heart muscle itself. Obviously, the heart muscle needs a lot of energy to keep the heart pumping, and high energy comes from good nutrition. If our arteries get clogged, or corroded like home plumbing which slows down sink drainage, blood flow will be slowed down; the heart will have to pump harder, and if a clot appears in the clogged artery, the blood flow may be stopped altogether.

When the blood cannot get through to the heart muscle and deliver to it the necessary food and oxygen to keep it alive, the heart-muscle cells will eventually die and the heart will not have the muscle to keep pumping. If the heart-muscle cells are sufficiently starved for the oxygen which is carried by the blood, the result is what is commonly referred to as a "coronary." We may have the healthiest blood possible, but if it can't get through to "deliver the goods," it's not of much use. This is one reason that physicians worry about excessively high cholesterol count, because cholesterol is a fatty substance which clogs up the arteries and slows down the circulation of the blood, making nutrition of the heart muscle more difficult.

How important is calcium to adult bone cells?

Your skeleton is the framing for your body. It enables you to move around and provides, in some instances, armor for vital organs such as the brain. Every mother knows that her baby requires milk, and she probably has been told by her doctor that milk is essential to strong bones. As the child grows, she is told to continue giving him several glasses of milk a day, in addition to his other foods. One of the main reasons for the emphasis on milk in the growing child's diet is that milk is a ready supply of calcium and protein. Bone is largely mineral in composition, mostly calcium phosphates, interlaced into a protein base. You would assume that once you had reached your mature physical development, nutrition for bones would decrease in importance. This was once thought to be essentially true, but today we know better.

When you break an arm, leg, collarbone, or any other bone, you assume that once the bone has been set by the physician that it must knit or mend. If your bone cells were dead, the bone would never mend. If bones knit relatively slowly, poor nutrition may be the cause, since minerals are constantly entering and leaving your bones. We know that bone repair can be slowed by poor nutrition and stepped up by improving nutrition. If you are hospitalized with a broken bone, you will notice that your diet will contain, in perhaps larger than usual quantities, those essentials for bone-cell nutrition. Since bone cells are alive, they need not only the materials necessary for bone building but all the other nutrients that other living cells need in order to stay alive. It is, therefore, advisable to continue to get some calcium in the adult diet.

What about the needs of my skin and hair?

In our study of laboratory animals, we have observed not only what goes on inside the animals, but we have studied their exterior cells of skin and hair. Both skin and hair are, in large part, dependent upon nutrition for healthy growth. There are also environmental elements which can affect these cells, such as sunlight, wind, cold, heat, etc., but good nutrition is essential to healthy hair and skin cells free of disease.

The cause and treatment of many skin and hair problems is still unknown, but there are certain diseases and conditions of the skin and hair which can be laid directly to dietary deficiencies.

Animal owners know that the condition of their pet's coat is an indication of his general well-being. If a dog or cat's coat is dry and dull with thin patches, instead of glossy and thick, you almost immediately surmise that something is wrong with his diet. Undoubtedly, a veterinarian will tell you the animal is suffering from a nutritional deficiency and advise adding the proper supplements to his diet.

Similarly, with people, many poor skin and hair conditions are symptomatic of nutritional deficiencies. For example, pellagra, a disease at one time not uncommon in the Southern states, results in a skin rash when the skin is exposed to the sun or to mild soap. The disease occurs when there is a lack of niacin, part of the Vitamin B-complex. A sufficient lack of B_2, known as riboflavin, will cause inflamed areas at the corners of the mouth. This is not to say that if a red spot appears at the corner of one's mouth he is definitely suffering from B_2 undernourishment, but the possibility is there and should not be ignored.

There is no doubt that all vitamins and minerals combine to influence the condition of your hair. Vitamins A, C, and E are very important, and within the B-complex group we have inositol, folic acid, para-aminobenzoic acid, and calcium pantothenate. Iron, copper, cobalt, and iodine are the most essential minerals. B-complex vitamins improve hair condition, and Vitamin B_2 is particularly important for the health of the scalp, as are Vitamins A and C. When Vitamin E was not included in the diet of experimental animals, baldness occurred in some.

Frequent skin infections may prove a Vitamin A deficiency. Dr. Roger Williams, again in his book, *Nutrition in a Nutshell,* says:

> The skin is a region which is known to be affected by many nutritional lacks. Scarcely a deficiency exists which does not manifest itself by pathological changes in the skin. This has been demonstrated particularly in animals, where it is possible to carry out conclusive experiments. The number of reports of human diseased-skin conditions that are improved by supplying deficient nutrients is large. . . . there is evidence that acne, eczemas, dermatitis (a general term for skin inflammation), and even psoriasis (a condition which is almost, by definition, mysterious and incurable) may in specific cases have a nutritional origin. Acne usually involves infections, but well-nourished skin appears to be able to resist such infections. Eczemas and rashes may have many causes but they are often completely eliminated as a result of better nutrition. Reliable reports of cases in which conditions diagnosed as psoriasis have been eliminated by the use of nutritional supplements, have been published.

He goes on to say,

> Among the many nutrients that have been implicated in diseased conditions of the skin and hair are vitamin A, vitamin D, vitamin E, vitamin C, thiamin, riboflavin, pantothenic acid, biotin, vitamin B_6, unsaturated 'fat acids, inositol, para-aminobenzoic acid, and essential amino acids.

and "Even this is not an exhaustive list." Allergies, chilblains, wound healing, and "the burning-foot syndrome" all involve the skin and its allied structures.

Abnormally dry hair and skin may signal a thyroid hormone deficiency and may also indicate the possibility of rheumatoid arthritis.

Should I take vitamin pills?

It does not behoove the layman to self-diagnose or to rush

to the local pharmacy for vitamin pills. Your body has certain self-regulating mechanisms within it and will not use nutrients which are not needed, so you may be wasting considerable money by taking vitamin pills which your system does not need. Furthermore, only a physician can decide just which vitamin and how many units of it you need.

It cannot be emphasized too strongly that popping vitamin pills into your mouth indiscriminately can be dangerous, just as is the use of other unprescribed medicine. For example, there has been a great deal of publicity lately about Nobel-prize winner Linus Pauling's recommendation for massive doses of Vitamin C to combat the common cold. Medical science has known for many years that Vitamin C does, in fact, help to keep a person free of colds, but massive doses taken without the advice of a physician can be dangerous, particularly to those suffering from gouty arthritis or diabetes, for example. In the case of diabetics, it can cause a person to miscalculate his daily dosage of insulin and this, of course, could be fatal.

What is the single most important thing I can do for my body?

Keep in mind that cellular malnutrition is the basis of all malnutrition. It is probably at the root of many, many more diseases or conditions than those mentioned. To prevent this damaging malnutrition, a well-balanced diet is most important, and this is why you must pay close attention to the food you eat.

Here are some charts to help you choose the proper foods.

The Vitamins, the Food We Eat, and Their Uses

The Vitamins*	The Food We Eat	Uses (Promotion, Treatment, Activation, Creation)	(Helps In Prevention Of)
Vitamin A	Carrots Liver, Lamb Spinach	Prom. Resistance to Infection, Healthy Skin, Normal Reproduction, Good Vision	Night Blindness; Eye Problems; Sensitivity to Light
Vitamin C (Ascorbic Acid)	Broccoli, Leaf Peppers, Green Lamb's Quarters	Prom. Healthy Tendons and Other Supporting Connective Tissue; Bone Knitting	Scurvy; Tooth Decay; Pyorrhea; Colds; Infections
Vitamin D	Cod-Liver Oil Milk (Sunshine)	Prom. Good Bone and Tooth Formation; Energy	Bone and Tooth Deformation; Fatigue
Vitamin D3 (Dehydrocholesterol)	Cod-Liver Oil Halibut-Liver Oil (Sunshine)		Rickets
Vitamin E (Tocopherols)	Corn Oil Wheat Germ Sweet Potatoes	Prom. Normal Fertility; Aids Successful Pregnancy	Heart Disease; Muscular Disorders
Vitamin K (Prothrombin)	Bright Green Leaves	Prom. Blood Clotting	Hemorrhage
Vitamin P	Grapes Oranges Lemons	Treat. Rheumatic Fever, Coronaries, Bursitis, Arthritis, Respiratory Infections	Miscarriage

84

Vitamin	Sources	Promotes / Treats	Deficiency Symptoms
Vitamin U	Cabbage Juice Egg Yolks, Raw Celery	Treat. Ulcers	
Vitamin B₁ (Thiamin)	Flour, Whole Wheat Kidney, Stewed Yeast		Beriberi; Heart Disease; Constipation
Vitamin B₂ (Riboflavin)	Kidney Stew Liver, Beef, Milk, Skim	Prom. Good Health; Vitality	Oily Skin; Dimness of Vision; Keratitis
(Niacin)	Beef Steak Chicken, Stewed Mushrooms	Prom. Good Health; Mental and Physical Well-Being	Pellagra; Diarrhea; Dermatitis; Dementia
Vitamin B₆ (Pyridoxine)	Liver Yeast, Brewer's Wheat Germ	Treat. Palsy (Parkinson's Disease)	Dizziness; Morning Sickness; Nausea in Pregnancy; Motion Sickness; Excessively Oily Skin
(Pantothenic Acid)	Egg Yolk Molasses Liver	Prom. Normal Growth	Skin Infections; Premature Aging; Loss of Hair
(Para-Amino-Benzoic Acid)	Liver, Rice Yeast	Prom. Retention of Hair Color	Gray Hair
Vitamin B₁₂	Grapefruit Yeast, Brewer's Wheat Germ	Prom. Growth and Color of Hair; Normal Intestinal Activity	Hardening of Arteries; Hair Color Loss

	The Food We Eat	Uses (Promotion, Treatment, Activation, Creation)	(Helps In Prevention Of)
(Choline)	Egg Yolk Yeast, Brewer's Liver, Beef		Arteriosclerosis; Chest Pain; Stroke
(Biotin)	Banana Milk, Raw Egg		Nausea; Muscular Pain; Heart Disturbance; Depression; Dry Peeling Skin; Gray Skin; Anorexia
(Folic Acid)	Liver Spinach Mushrooms	Treat. Pernicious Anemia	Paleness; Fatigue; Lassitude; Anemia
Vitamin B14	All B-Rich Foods	Act. Bone Marrow to Produce New Blood Cells	
Vitamin B15 (Pangamic Acid)	Liver Yeast, Brewer's Rice Bran	Creat. Creatine (Important to Muscular Acivity)	Muscular Disorders

* Vitamin B-Complex Table on next page.

The Minerals, the Food We Eat, and Their Uses

The Minerals	The Food We Eat	Uses (Promotion, Treatment, Activation, Creation)	(Helps In Prevention Of)
Calcium	Milk, Skim, Dry, Powdered; Buttermilk Cheese, American	Prom. Good Muscle Tone	Tooth Decay; Bone Fragility Cramps; Nervousness

Mineral	Food Sources	Function	Deficiency Symptoms
Phosphorus	Cottage Cheese Flour, Whole Rye Milk, Skim, Dry, Powdered	Prom. Good Bone and Tooth Formation, Muscular Contraction, Growth	Rickets; Imperfect Teeth; Bad Appetite; Weight Loss; Generalized Weakness
Iron	Apricots, Dried Clams Flour, Whole Wheat		Anemia; Fatigue; Pale Skin; Dull Hair; Mental Confusion
Iodine	Oysters Eggs Spinach	Treat. Thyroid Disorders	Goiter
Copper	Liver Molasses Apricots, Dried	Treat. Undulant Fever	Anemia; Gray Hair; Generalized Weakness; Impaired Respiration
Sodium	Salt Muscle, Animal Vegetables, All	Prom. Good Growth	Thinness; Muscular Shrinkage; Gas; Lung Infection; Blindness
Potassium	Grains, Whole; Figs Potatoes; Tomatoes Citrus Fruit	Prom. Good Health, Growth	Nervousness; Constipation; Insomnia; Heart-Muscle Damage, Kidney Damage; Brittle Bones
Chlorine	Salt, Table Meat, Raw Milk		Slowing of Growth; Loss of Hair; Apprehension & Fear; Eye, Mouth, Nose Hemorrhage

87

	The Food We Eat	Uses	
Manganese	Leaves, Green; Beets; Egg Yolk	Prom. Good Bone Growth, Normal Pregnancy	Stillbirth; Bone Deformation
Magnesium	Nuts; Egg Yolks; Oranges		Low Blood Pressure; Irritability; Nervousness; Convulsions; Rapid Heart Beat
Cobalt	Lentils; Buckwheat; Mushrooms	Treat. Undulant Fever	Anemia; Listlessness; Emaciation; Undulant Fever
Sulphur	Cabbage; Brussels Sprouts; Molasses	Prom. Beauty of Skin, Hair, Fingernails	Poor Skin; Dull Hair; Soft and Cracking Fingernails

Essential Amino Acids, the Food We Eat, and Their Uses

Essential Amino Acids	The Food We Eat	Uses (Promotion, Treatment, Activation, Creation)	(Helps In Prevention Of)
Histidine	Cheese; Beef Heart; Peanuts	Prom. Good Growth and Healing	Slow Wound Healing
Isoleucine	Milk, Cow's; Mussels; Yeast	Prom. Healthy Liver Metabolism	Liver Disorders

Amino Acid	Sources	Function	Disorders
Leucine	Beef Muscle, Sardines, Rolled Oats	Production of Urea (Liver Function)	Liver Disorders
Lysine	Cheese, Mussels, Yeast	Prom. Good Growth, Healthy Blood, Reproduction	Retarded Growth; Anemia; Reproduction Problems; Pneumonia; Acidosis; Bloodshot Eyes
Methionine	Eggs, Beef Liver, Corn	Prom. Good Hair Growth, Liver and Heart Function, Normal Pregnancy	Baldness; Liver Degeneration; Rheumatic Fever; Toxemia in Pregnancy
Phenylalanine	Cheese, Beef Brain, Rice	Production of Thyroxin (required for Normal Thyroid Function) and of Epinephrine (Essential for Heart and Blood Vessel Function)	Thyroid Disorders; Bloodshot Eyes; Cataracts; Nervousness
Tryptophane	Milk, Cow's, Sesame, Beet Tops	Prom. Proper Development Tooth Enamel; Normal Growth; Good Digestive Function; Steady Nerves	Thinness; Hair Loss; Bloodshot Eyes; Skin Problems; Digestive Upsets; Nervous Disorders; Cataracts; Blindness
Threonine	Eggs, Mussels, Yeast	Prom. Healthy Liver Function	Liver Disorders
Valine	Milk, Cow's, Peanuts, Rolled Oats	Prom. Proper Nervous System Function	Nervous Disorders

9

What Is a Fad Diet?

Do fad diets have an optimal amount of nutrients?

A fad diet is any currently popular "crash" diet designed for quick weight loss and not supervised by a doctor. Usually the dieter eats a high proportion of one category of food. By definition, the fad diet excludes the other nutrients necessary for maintaining a healthy body while losing weight.

What in our modern life makes losing weight so difficult and, in turn, attracts people to fad diets?

For the past several years, fad dieting has become a way of life for millions of Americans—men, women, and children. It is hardly surprising in this affluent, overweight society which, through the mass media, glamorizes youth, vitality, and fashion-plate figures for both men and women.

Dieters know intellectually that it is wrong and dangerous to diet without medical supervision, but the well-planned diet of the nutrition-oriented physician limits weight loss to between one and two pounds a week; is it any wonder that the woman attempting to take off thirty pounds in six weeks so that she can appear at her daughter's wedding in a size-ten dress strikes out on her own with the help of any number of "paperbacks" or magazine articles?

Magazine readers are constantly plagued and titillated by the promise on the cover "to take off ten pounds in two weeks" with one or another diet dreamed up to sell magazines. The inconsistency lies in the fact that along with the diet and the plea to the reader to diet for health reasons— the avoidance of a coronary attack, diabetes onset, arthritic pain, etc.—are pages upon pages of advertisements advertising luscious, high-calorie foods topped with whipped cream. If advertising is to be effective, it must make the reader want to buy or eat the product. Dieting is difficult enough for any person who enjoys eating without being further assaulted by advertising which seems determined to counteract any dieter's best intentions.

It is no secret that our so-called "modern" way of life is the culprit in countless overweight problems. We walk hardly at all and, in general, our physical activity does not remotely approximate that of past generations. The influence of television has not only adversely affected the condition of the overweight adult but that of the younger generation also. Today, thousands of families clear the dinner table only to sit down in front of their television sets and begin munching on sweets and other snacks, usually high in carbohydrate, until they go to bed. It is no wonder that most of these television habitués soon wake up to find that their waistlines have expanded by several inches. The habit has become so widespread that the food industry has latched on to it and now confidently advertises certain foods as "TV snacks"!

P. W., a forty-two-year-old man, was a victim of this modern cultural pattern. Quite without realizing it, he had got into the habit of munching while watching television from after dinner time until he went to bed.

During this period of physical inactivity, he had gained eighteen pounds in excess of his ideal weight. Laboratory tests showed that his blood sugar was below normal and, in fact, he was suffering from a not uncommon condition known as hypoglycemia (low blood sugar). This condition results in a craving for sweets, the body's attempt to provide the sugar which is lacking. However, the result of stuffing one's body with sweets is that the pancreas responds by putting out more and more insulin, which will not allow the blood sugar to increase to a normal level. It is a vicious cycle.

To break the cycle, the patient was put on the appropriate diet for his condition, a high-protein low-*proportionate*-carbohydrate diet. Within six weeks, he had lost the eighteen excess pounds and his blood sugar returned to normal. He has maintained his ideal weight for approximately four years.

Can I lose weight both quickly and safely?

It is natural and understandable that if you have thirty to one hundred pounds to shed you want to do it in the quickest way possible, so you convince yourself that using a crash diet will accomplish the goal in the shortest time. The sad truth is that there is no panacea for quick weight loss. There are, indeed, ways of taking off weight more quickly than other ways, but these methods, to be successful, must certainly be used under close medical supervision. For example, prolonged fasting can be very effective, but *under no circumstances* should it be attempted unless the faster is in a hospital under direct observation by a physician. Drastic measures very often produce drastic results; and unless your chemistry is closely checked during drastic diets, it is quite possible for you to end up with serious damage to one or more of the vital organs.

If I lose weight very quickly by crash dieting will it be a permanent loss?

It is not difficult for you to diagnose yourself as overweight or even obese; but it is outside your capability to diagnose accurately the causes of your weight problem. For this reason, there are countless people who go on crash diets to little or no avail. They half-starve themselves, both quantitatively and nutritionally, and lose weight only to gain it back, usually with additional poundage.

Most fad diets limit the dieter to one or two foods, so you get too much of one kind of nutrient and not enough of others. Three things make it extremely difficult to maintain a long-term weight loss this way. First, you have no well-balanced dietary guidelines by which to revise your eating habits; without these it is almost impossible to maintain healthy low weight. Second, this fad-diet limitation on kinds of nutrients tends to throw your system out of balance. Once the body is out of balance, it is difficult to set it on a straight course again. For this reason, many people lose weight and then gain it back, because by the time they resume regular eating again, their metabolic systems are not behaving normally and their bodies may be storing considerable fat, simply because their food is not being used or burned up properly.

There is another, or third supporting reason why weight lost by crash dieting isn't likely to stay lost. Recent studies show conclusively that not all obesity is caused simply by overeating, although in most instances this may have triggered it. Just as metabolic disorders play a role in obesity, so does heredity. These subjects are dealt with in more detail in Chapter 15.

Some doctors use "high-protein" diets. Are these fad diets? Now let us analyze each of several popular fad diets. To begin with, let's examine the "high-protein" diet, which is extremely popular. If you examine most physicians' diets, you will note that providing you are a healthy individual, they contain a high proportion of protein to carbohydrate; however, they are not diets devoid of carbohydrate nor are they lacking in any other nutritional essentials. They are well-balanced diets.

What is the main danger of the popular "high-protein" diet?

In the popular, or fad "high-protein" diet, you eat practically nothing but meat, cheese, eggs, etc., in some instances swilled down with generous amounts of Martinis, bourbon on the rocks, and other alcoholic drinks (except beer, which happens to have a high carbohydrate content). If you embark on the "high-protein" diet and, unhappily, are unaware of a kidney infection or malfunction, it is conceivable that you might retain urea, lapse into a coma, and die. This is, of course, the most extreme possibility, but in any case, this diet, without the proper supplements, is eventually only going to compound the problem.

What are the dangers of a "low-carbohydrate" diet?

Another popular diet is the "low-carbohydrate" diet. There are some people whose bodies demand an amount of carbohydrate which might be slightly higher than what is considered the minimum requirement for "normals." These people may develop hypoglycemia if they do not have the proper amount of carbohydrates. Because such a person has a lower concentration of glucose or of sugar in the circulating blood, his brain is not properly nourished, nor is the retina of the eye. People with hypoglycemia (low sugar) complain of their mental efficiency being slowed down, dizziness, fatigue, extreme irritability, and, in advanced cases, the possibility of loss of sight; indeed, even death can result. Only your doctor can determine how much carbohydrate you must have in your diet. Again, you must always remember that no two people are exactly alike, not even identical twins. Therefore, people foolish enough to practice self-diagnosis and follow "low-carbohydrate" fad diets may be headed for serious trouble. Too often, these rage diets are not only low in carbohydrate, but also in essential nutrients.

If this is true of the "low-carbohydrate" diets, what occurs in "high-carbohydrate" diets?

For the patient who is already suffering from hypoglycemia, too much carbohydrate in the diet can be equally dangerous.

Let's look at the history of B. P., a forty-one-year-old woman who had had a weight problem throughout her adult life. She had gone on crash diets more than twelve times and estimated that she had gained and lost over five hundred pounds during her lifetime. The last fad diet that she had tried was what she termed the drinking-man's diet (a high-carbohydrate diet, unlike the published "drinking-man's diet," which is low in carbohydrate and high in protein).

In the first week of this latest fad diet, she lost fifteen pounds; the second week, she lost six pounds; and then she began to suffer from headaches, dizzy spells, sleeplessness and occasional fainting spells. Despite these problems, she stayed on the same diet and then gained four pounds. She continued to regain, and by the time she sought help and was referred to me, she was thirty-five pounds overweight.

A thorough physical examination and laboratory tests showed her to be suffering from low blood sugar. Further tests revealed that a tumor of the islet cells of the pancreas, the insulin-producing area, was the culprit. The patient was operated upon and the tumor removed. During the ensuing four months, her abnormal symptoms of headaches, dizziness, sleeplessness, and fainting spells disappeared, and she achieved her normal weight.

This case is a clear example of what the wrong kind of diet can do to the unsuspecting person. When she went on the high-carbohydrate diet, she was actually causing her abnormal pancreas to secrete more insulin, which burned up the sugar at such a rate that her blood sugar fell to dangerously low levels. This produced hypoglycemia which resulted in her having an abnormal craving for sweets and foods high in carbohydrate.

It is now more than two years since her surgery, and she has kept well and has maintained her weight.

It can be easily demonstrated that the effect of a diet on Person A, for example, may be completely different from its effect on Person B. In the previous case, we showed how a high-carbohydrate diet aggravated an already existing condition. In this case, it was hypoglycemia caused by a tumor of the pancreas. In the case of T. Z., a forty-one-year-old man who had been on the identical diet, the results and symptoms were quite different.

Mr. T. Z. had been crash dieting for seven years and was forty-one pounds over his desired weight when he was first examined by me. He had noticed that each time he dieted he lost and then regained the weight lost, plus gaining additional weight. His latest diet had been the same high-carbohydrate diet along with considerable quantities of alcohol. Unlike B. P., T. Z. felt fine, except for being troubled by his weight increase and a certain "psychological-sociological up-tightness."

Physical examination showed that the patient's blood pressure was a little high, and blood studies showed a high cholesterol count, plus a high level of other fats in the blood (triglycerides). His physiological problem was diagnosed as a primary hypertriglyceridemia (too much fatty substance in the blood). The patient was put on a special diet which restricted his carbohydrate intake, and specified unsaturated fats with a minimum of saturated fats. Because of his elevated cholesterol, the patient was advised to use a diet low in animal fats and was told to avoid all dairy products except for skim milk; to select foods made with skim milk; and to substitute margarine rich in unhydrogenated vegetable oils for butter. He was told not to use olive oil or peanut oil in salads, because both these oils are high in cholesterol.

The patient received a particular medication to activate

the mechanism which enables the body to excrete fatty substances. Within eight months, his cholesterol, triglyceride, blood pressure, and weight had all returned to normal. He was also encouraged to engage in regular exercise, avoid cigarette smoking, and, when possible, to reduce psychological-social stresses. Fortunately, he has been able to accomplish these goals and has remained well over the past six years.

What are the dangers of a "high-fat" fad diet?

The "high-fat" fad diet, while not highly palatable, except possibly to Eskimos, is as risky as it is distasteful. Overabundance of fat in the diet can cause diarrhea. Constant diarrhea will cause weight loss because if the food is constantly being expelled from the body, it has little or no chance to be absorbed. This might seem to be a painful but quick way to lose weight (it can also be accomplished by constant use of cathartics). But what happens when one is plagued by daily diarrhea? In the first place, it can cause a loss of essential vitamins, minerals, and cofactors (compounds essential for the functioning of enzymes). Loss of fluid is also a danger, for serious dehydration indicates that the body cells are being depleted of the fluids which they need for survival. Necessary electrolytes, such as magnesium, potassium, and sodium, are lost; and if the fluids and other essential elements are not replaced fairly quickly, coma and death can result.

If "high-fat" diets are bad, does this make "low-fat" diets good?

No. A diet which is too *low* in fats can also be harmful. There are three essential fats which the body is not able to manufacture, and therefore, must be included in the daily diet. If these fats are not present, the result may be dry skin and scalp, decreased lubrication in the joints, etc. Furthermore, fats are an essential building material for creating and sustaining life. They provide us with our most concentrated form of energy, and they combine with phosphorus to form part of every cell. Fats are particularly concentrated in nerve and brain tissues. Under your skin, there is a padding of fat which serves as cushioning for nerves and muscles and which helps to protect the body from sudden changes of temperature. Three of the vital organs, kidneys, heart, and liver, are supported by a small bed of fat.

It has been shown with experimental animals that when a diet is completely fat free, the animals become emaciated, and develop skin rashes and kidney disorders. Two researchers, Drs. William Cooper and James Hart, of the Lee Foundation for Nutritional Research in Milwaukee, Wisconsin, report that the essential fats are needed for all glandular health, and particularly for healthy prostate glands in men.

Can too much of any one food be fattening?

It may come as something of a surprise to many readers to learn that too much of *any one* food can, indeed, prove to be fattening—even protein. The case of P. J., a forty-one-year-old woman, clearly demonstrates this point.

Over a period of fifteen years, P. J. had lost and gained a total of some four hundred pounds and clearly indicated the Yo-Yo Syndrome.

She had always had a lean upper body but was obese in the hips, thighs, and legs. At the time of her examination by me, she complained about becoming too easily fatigued, being cold in winter, and having dry skin.

She admitted to having attended a diet club where she was placed on a diet allowing an unlimited amount of protein. During the first week, she lost eleven pounds and then an additional six pounds in the second week. Naturally, she was elated with her rapid weight loss, but she was in for a bitter disappointment at the end of the third week. By then, she had gained back eight of the lost pounds, and, at the end of the month, had gained another ten pounds. The net result was, in fact, after a month of strenuous dieting, a gain of one pound. Not very encouraging!

She further admitted to me that she used an excessive amount of salt in her diet. This, of course, resulted in abnormal retention of body fluids and swelling of the legs.

Without consulting a physician, she began taking a diuretic which a well-meaning "friend" provided. When the diuretic did not work as well as she hoped, she doubled the dose! Still dissatisfied with the results, she eventually was taking three diuretic pills a day. At this point, one might be tempted to say, "Heavens, what a stupid woman." Certainly, she did not use good judgment in taking medicines without advice from her physician, but unhappily, she is not an isolated case. Too many persons endanger their lives by taking "a friend's" medicine.

The result of this poor judgment was the development of a tingling sensation in her fingers and toes, and finally, nausea and loss of consciousness.

When P. J. was first seen by me, she was fifty-one pounds over her recommended weight. Laboratory tests showed that her excessive use of the unprescribed diuretics had caused her to lose potassium and to become deficient in this essential electrolyte.

Her type of obesity—thin from the waist up and fat from the waist down—indicated a condition in which a person's body does not properly metabolize fat. In medicine, it is referred to as *lipodystrophy*.

After treatment for the acute episode, the patient was placed on a well-balanced diet containing sufficient potassium in the foods, and within ten months, she had reduced herself to her ideal weight and has stayed near that level for the past eight years. The indiscriminate use of diuretics was, of course, stopped.

P. J.'s case is a fine illustration of how too much of any kind of food is fattening. The human body has limited storage for protein, so excessive protein will then be converted into excessive weight; or, through a process known as gluconeogenesis, the protein will be converted by the body into excessive sugar.

P. J. was lucky that she got into competent medical hands before it was too late. Had her potassium loss continued, death most certainly would have ensued—and needlessly.

What are "rainbow pills" and can they hurt me?

There have been, in the past few years, medical as well as newspaper accounts of persons dying from the combined use of "rainbow pills"—diuretics, digitalis, and thyroid extracts. In these instances, the symptoms were those of an overdose of digitalis, and a combination of medical problems; the loss of body potassium and heart irregularities resulted in death. All drugs should be administered only under the direction of a competent physician. The Food and Drug Administration has outlawed "rainbow pills" for the treatment of obesity.

I have heard of the "macrobiotic diet." What is it?

Another popular fad diet is the "macrobiotic diet" which, in its purest form, is a combination of sesame seed, sea water, and seaweed. This diet lacks B vitamins, an essential amino acid, and is, in fact, *not* compatible with life over long periods of time.

There has been more than one death reported because of this diet, particularly among young men and women.

Is there any good that can be said for fad diets?

Probably the only saving grace in the case of fad diets is that they are often not very palatable, are tasteless, dull, and boring; so the dieter rarely sticks them out for very long. Unfortunately, once in a while, a highly motivated strong-minded person gets hooked on one of these with serious, and sometimes fatal results.

Could not then a "perfect supplement" be added to fad diets to make them nutritionally safe?

The following chapter will answer your question.

10

The Perfect Supplement

You said that the "macrobiotic diet" had resulted in death for the dieter. Could a supplement to this fad diet have prevented this from happening?

A twenty-four-year-old Clifton, New Jersey, woman died not long ago after subsisting for about ten months on a Zen Buddhist "macrobiotic diet" consisting of natural cereals three times a day, as little water as possible, and gomasio, which is four parts sesame seed sprinkled with one part sea salt.

Ironically, the word "macrobiotic" means "tending to prolong life." Equally ironic is the fact that the young lady dropped from the 130 pounds she weighed when she went on the diet, to slightly over seventy pounds at the time of her death.

A tragedy? Of course. But a tragedy that today medical science could prevent with its knowledge of a new, safe diet supplement. Unfortunately, it has come too late to save that particular young woman. If it had been available, and if the young woman had protected herself with it and eaten adequate protein (in her case, slightly more than one ounce daily), she would not have died but would have continued to enjoy sound, if somewhat emaciated looking, health.

Can a fad or crash diet harm me, and if so, how?

Yes. To understand how this can be, let's consider a few basic facts about nutrition and dieting. First, the big gamble with fad or crash diets has never been whether or not they will make you lose weight; the craziest of them will do that, often with dramatic speed: vinegar; French boiled egg; liquid; Air Force; Mayo Clinic (rightly disavowed by the famous Minnesota Medical Center, which had nothing to do with the diet); drinking-man's; high-protein; rice; meal-skipping. You name it; you use it; you'll shed pounds—for a while.

But then (if you're lucky and don't succumb like the young woman mentioned above) the pounds all come surging back. Somehow, with fad diets, the glory of being slender and feeling fit rarely lasts. But there is a much more hazardous side to crash dieting than the return of poundage. It is the problem, little understood by most people, but potentially lethal, of what *else* you're shedding on one of these diets besides fat; or *instead of* fat.

For on the wrong kind of diet, it isn't the excess fat that your body's metabolism (or "chemical-furnace" system) attacks to break it down into energy; instead, such ill-conceived diets bypass the intended effect of fat reduction and by a kind of short-circuiting of metabolic processes destroy muscle and organ tissue. You cannot afford to lose much of these kinds of tissue because some of it, brain tissue, for example, is irreplaceable.

Fad or crash dieting is like trying to run an expensive engine on French perfume. It will run at first because of the alcohol, but the oils and aromatics will soon make it run raggedly, and eventually it will stall, its exquisitely machined parts a mess beyond repair. So also with fad diets and reckless dieters.

Does it concern you that the latest dietary brainstorm of some dubiously qualified nutritional "expert" can cost you dearly, can mean an ominous erosion of body components, such as heart, kidney, liver, brain, and over-all musculature?

It should, for that is what happens to you on a nutritionally inadequate diet; you lose weight, all right, but by shedding precious muscle and organ tissue rather than fat. You literally wear away at the cellular level in a slow, inexorable manner. On such a regimen, you undergo an insidiously accelerated dying process at the core of your physical being. No wonder some of these horrible diets leave you feeling dragged out, on edge, shaky, or worse. *There is absolutely no fad or crash diet which, from the scientific standpoint, is nutritionally adequate.*

Could I be fat on the outside yet be starving on the inside?

Yes; one of the main purposes of my research at The Johns Hopkins Hospital and the University of Maryland School of Medicine has been to find a way to maintain a healthy bodyweight range for people who have overweight problems. During my years of laboratory and clinical research, I have concluded that many overweight and obese people are overfed yet undernourished. This is a national problem. Very often, improper body metabolism is due to poor nutrition, fad diets, and overmedication early in life. I believe that the body, in later life, reacts, as I have said, with a kind of "Yo-Yo response" wherein the body weight swings high, responds to a crash diet for a time, but then regains the lost weight, often with a few additional pounds, and the problem begins all over again.

I am concerned that my children, who are "picky," won't get optimal nutrition. Is my concern justified?

Yes, it is. Data from my recent research study showed that approximately one-half of all people I interviewed were not receiving the recommended daily allowances of dietary vitamins and/or amino acids and/or minerals. These statistics were recently confirmed by a government survey.

For some time, it has been the hope of nutritionists that

a single formula could be perfected which could contain all the basic minimum requirements of vitamins, amino acids, and minerals to promote good health in humans. Now, after many years of work, we have achieved such a formula. This perfect supplement is now in the process of being patented.

Just what is this perfect supplement?

The perfect supplement is a nutritional substance composed of the recommended dietary allowances of vitamins and minerals. It also contains adequate protein and/or the essential amino acids. The supplement, taken once a day, with adequate calories, provides the cofactors necessary for normal metabolism and acts as a metabolic normalizer.

The formula was determined by reviewing the world's pertinent medical literature and then, as a result of accepting some and rejecting other data based on my critical analysis of same, developing requirements for vitamins, amino acids, and minerals for the maintenance of good nutrition of practically all healthy humans.

In certain cases, the data reviewed were not sufficient, and therefore, I had to extrapolate from the textual material. It also became obvious that the requirements were different for the following six groups; thus, the requirements for six different groups are so formulated. These specific groups, from a nutritional standpoint, are:

1. infants (up to twelve months of age);
2. children (from twelve months to ten years);
3. adult males (from ten years up);
4. adult females (from ten years up);
5. pregnant women; and
6. lactating women.

Living organisms, in contrast to inanimate matter, require nutritive processes. Identifiable nutrients must be present in specific proportions characteristic to the species, so that the necessary functions of digestion, absorption, metabolism, and excretion for generative and regenerative cycles may continue at all times.

Recommended dietary allowances have been tabulated for calories, protein, calcium, phosphorus, iodine, magnesium, iron, Vitamin A, thiamine, riboflavin, niacin, ascorbic acid, Vitamin D, Vitamin E, folacin, Vitamin B_6, and Vitamin B_{12}. The recommended dietary allowances of vitamins and minerals are very similar to those established by the Food and Nutrition Board of the National Research Council. Although they have not been tabulated, other nutrients, such as Vitamin K, biotin, choline, pantothenic acid, copper, fluorine, chromium, cobalt, manganese, molybdenum, selenium, zinc, water, sodium, potassium, and chloride are necessary to the human for the process of nutrition.

Is it true that people are burning up less calories today than they did, say, ten years ago?

Caloric recommendations are based on the required amount of energy needed for the rate of growth at optimal levels and to maintain body weight. Of course, caloric levels for children must allow for growth and development. However, caloric allowances for adults reflect the resting metabolic rate as well as body size and energy expenditure. It is interesting to note that in the last ten years, the average daily caloric allowance has dropped, for men, from 3,200 to 2,800, and, for women, from 2,300 to 2,000.

From what do I derive most of my energy?

In the United States, carbohydrates and fats, which are the major sources of food energy, account for forty-seven per cent and forty-one per cent, respectively, of the total caloric intake. Protein, which accounts for only twelve per cent of the daily caloric consumption, is needed to compensate for endogenous losses as well as to provide for the requirements of growth and pregnancy. Body protein is composed of twenty amino acids. Nine of these are called essential amino acids and are obtainable solely through dietary protein, which also provides the nitrogen necessary for body-protein synthesis. With adequate calorie consumption, it is difficult not to meet minimal protein needs. However, on many crash diets, where protein is greatly restricted or in some cases eliminated, the intake of these essential amino acids can fall far below the daily requirements, resulting in loss of body protein and negative nitrogen balance. On the other hand, protein intake increased above the basic needs can serve as an extra energy source, which may account for the fact that those populations which consume considerable protein generally thrive better than those living on lower amounts.

What should I know about the various vitamins and minerals?

Vitamin A is present in foods available in the United States at about 7,500 I.U. (international units) per day. Half of this is generally obtained from oils, fats, meats, fish, eggs, and dairy products, and the other half from fruits and vegetables.

Vitamin D is added to milk and to certain other fluids, such as fruit drinks.

Vitamin E is available from plant oils, margarines, shortenings, and whole grains.

Ascorbic acid (Vitamin C) is required only by man, monkey, and guinea pigs for prevention of scurvy.

The recommended daily allowance of folacin is 0.4 mg. (milligram), far greater than the amount needed as a pure synthetic vitamin. This is due to the fact that there is some question about the availability of folacin in foods and its loss in cooking.

Niacin is obtained in most diets from fish, meat, and poultry, and twenty-five per cent comes from whole-grain and enriched flour and cereal products. It is needed to prevent pellagra.

The recommended allowances of riboflavin are based on body size, metabolism, and growth rates. The main sources of riboflavin are milk and cheese products, meat, eggs, and whole-grain and enriched flour and cereal products.

The recommended adult allowance of Vitamin B_6 is 2.1 mg. per day, and that of Vitamin B_{12} is 5.0 mcg. (micrograms) per day.

The main source of calcium is milk and milk products. Individual absorption of calcium varies greatly. The requirement for infants is proportionally greater than for adults.

Iodine is also required for humans. Iodized salt serves as one widely used source.

Balance studies indicate that 200 to 300 mg. (100 mg. per 1,000 K cal) of magnesium are necessary daily.

The absorption of iron varies widely from individual to individual. The amount recommended for adult women is almost twice that for men. It is difficult for women on an intake of 2,000 calories per day to meet their requirement, so their iron needs must be met through supplements.

These requirements can be translated into their sources in actual foods through the use of the charts in Chapter 8.

Who are the people most likely to be malnourished? Could I be one?

Yes, you could. The investigations of dieting and nutritional metabolism which led to the supplement formula began more than eight years ago, when I found that over fifty per cent of patients that I interviewed at the Johns Hopkins Hospital and Baltimore City Hospitals were not receiving their recommended daily allowances of vitamins, minerals, and/or protein as those requirements were then defined. I found that nutritional deficiency was exceptionally high in patients over the age of fifty, and was alarmingly prevalent in overweight patients who were on a variety of odd diets. Affluent patients who preferred cocktails, cookies, and candy to fruits and vegetables in their diet were another nutritionally deficient group, as were the people at the other end of the social scale, the very poor, who could afford only starchy, carbohydrate-laden foods, such as macaroni, potatoes, bread, and cereals, and hence suffered from protein deprivation.

What can be done about this situation?

At the outset of the investigation, which eventually included more than one thousand patients, I combed the medical literature having to do with nutritional work done in the field with animals and human beings, and then applied my findings in a program of carefully controlled research on my patients. My goal was to come up with a map of the metabolic pathways in nutrition. Working out the formula from such a map would then be just a simple matter of using slide rules.

The method of investigation was time-consuming, but scientifically indispensable. To understand it calls for a certain amount of sophisticated information that can help you in solving your own nutritional problems.

People who are malnourished because they can't help it (the poor), or don't know any better (the affluent), or because they are on some fad diet, suffer from what is scientifically called "negative nitrogen balance," which simply means that the body is putting out more nitrogen than it is taking in. When that happens, you are metabolically tearing down your own muscle and organ cells to extract energy content, faster than you are building up replacements for the cells. As a result, your body is no longer in "dynamic equilibrium."

Scientists can detect this state of affairs by careful "balanced studies," which consist of measuring the nitrogen you ingest and then subtracting the output in your urine and feces. I use nitrogen as my gauge of dynamic equilibrium. Nitrogen-balance studies are significant then, because I can give nitrogen to you in the foods of experimental diets and from your waste products get precise readings of whether or not your body is enjoying dynamic equilibrium; in other words, whether or not you are in good health.

Is this the method you used in your research to determine exactly how much of a nutrient a person needs?

Yes, this is exactly what was done with my patients. Through experimental diets, patients were given every known component of good nutrition, except one. That one item was then added to the diet in tiny amounts until it reached a level where continuous tests showed that the diet now prevented them from going into negative nitrogen balance. That level was often measured to the last milligram (one thousandth of a gram), and then they went to the next component to be assayed, gradually building that up to resolve its critical level for preventing negative nitrogen balance. In this way, I found the ideal combination of vitamins, amino acids, and minerals needed to sustain sound nutrition, in conjunction with a scant nine-tenths gram daily of protein per kilogram of ideal body weight. It was the basis for the perfect supplement formula.

Can the perfect supplement cure a vitamin deficiency?

No. There are limitations to what the supplement formula can do. There is a pronounced negative nitrogen balance in such cell-consuming disorders as cancer, leukemia, Cushing's Syndrome, etc., but it is not the kind of situation that the formula can do anything about, unfortunately. With such afflictions, the assault on the cellular constellations is just too massive, and *the supplement is designed to prevent negative nitrogen balance.*

What is the best way to get my needed nutrients?

The main thing to remember about nutrition is that ideally, you should get the vitamins, amino acids, and minerals you need *from your daily food.* Unfortunately, an amazing number of people do not get the basic nourishment they need from that source. This seems true no matter how "apparently balanced" the diets they enjoy, and it is true even in cases where people gorge themselves and become grossly overweight. Until these people arrive at a diet that is ideal for them and will keep them naturally in nitrogen balance, the supplement is the nutritional insurance they will need to do the job.

Can diseases caused by nutritional deficiency be prevented?

The supplement offers the solution that means an end to the nutritional-deficiency diseases that have plagued man throughout history: pellagra, beriberi, scurvy, and many others. It provides us with an effective, safe, reliable, inexpensive means of holding the line against those scourges until agricultural research heralds the day that nutritional scientists everywhere earnestly hope for—the day when nobody will need the supplement.

The new supplement formula is a relatively low-cost powdery substance which can be combined with ordinary food products, such as cereals, bread products, or milk. It can be a great boon in the prevention of malnutrition throughout the world.

The formula provides the basic nourishment needed to allow millions of people to diet sensibly and safely without the various ill effects that usually plague them. That, in itself, is something no diet pill known to medical science has ever allowed.

Private enterprise is now in the process of trying to convert this formula into the perfect supplement so that it can be added to one of our basic foods.

What are your recommended daily allowances of vitamins and minerals for adult men and women?

Recommended Daily Allowance

Vitamin/Mineral	Adult Men	Adult Women
Vitamin A	5,000 I.U.	5,000 I.U.
Vitamin B_6	2.1 mg.	2.1 mg.
Vitamin B_{12}	5 mcg.	5 mcg.

Thiamine	2.1 mg.	2.1 mg
Vitamin C (Ascorbic Acid)	60 mg.	55 mg.
Vitamin D	400 I.U.	400 I.U.
Vitamin E	30 I.U.	25 I.U.
Calcium	800 mg.	800 mg.*
Phosphorus	800 mg.	800 mg.*
Folacin	0.4 mg.	0.4 mg.
Iodine	100-150 mcg.	90-120 mcg.
Iron	10 mg.	18 mg.
Magnesium	300-350 mg.	300 mg.
Niacin	14-18 mg.	14-18 mg.
Riboflavin	1.7 mg.	1.5 mg.

NOTE: * Except during pregnancy when requirement increases.

What major diseases would be prevented by the use of the supplement? What are some symptoms of these diseases?

Diseases Prevented by the Vitamin Portion of the Perfect Supplement

Disease	Signs and Symptoms	Type of Deficiency
1. Xerophthalmia	Night Blindness; Skin Dryness	Vitamin A
2. Beriberi	Fatigue; Loss of Appetite; Nausea; Vomiting; Neuritis; Heart Disease; Brain Disease	Thiamine
3. Pellagra	Sore Tongue; Red, Itchy Skin; Mental Disorders	Niacin
4. Ariboflavinosis	Sore Mouth; Dermatosis; Eye Disease	Riboflavin
5. Mixed Syndromes of B₂ Avitaminosis	Paraplegia; Dermatitis	Nicotinic Acid and Riboflavin
6. Scurvy	Plugged-up Hair Follicles; Bleeding Gums; Fatigue	Vitamin C
7. Rickets	Poor Bone Formation	Vitamin D
8. Atocopherolosis	Heart Disease; Muscle Weakness	Vitamin E
9. Anaphtloquinonosis	Hemorrhage	Vitamin K

What people can benefit from the supplement? *

Are you among the many people who need it?

1. Those who cannot afford a balanced diet.
2. People who are unwilling to take the time to eat a variety of nourishing foods, have to eat away from home, make do with skimpy meals, or skip meals entirely.
3. People who eat for taste rather than for nutrition (and this includes many husbands and children).
4. Youngsters who dislike and avoid green vegetables and fruit.
5. Those people, one out of every three Americans, who are trying to lose weight by dieting, but fail to supplement the drastic cut in essential nutrients that dieting (especially fad or crash dieting) imposes.

What are the foods I would daily have to eat not to require the perfect supplement?

You do not need it if your daily diet includes:

1. One or more servings of leafy-green and yellow vegetables.
2. One or more servings of citrus fruit, tomatoes, raw cabbage.
3. Two or more servings of potatoes and other vegetables and fruits.
4. Two or more cups of milk (for children, three or four cups), or its equivalent in cheese, or ice cream.
5. One or two servings of meat, fish, poultry, eggs, dried peas, or beans.
6. Bread or cereals, whole-grain or enriched.
7. Butter or fortified margarine.

*Requirements are different for pregnant and lactating females—consult your physician.

11

Eating, Your Intelligence, and Your Well-Being

Do I have to eat the right things in order to enjoy good physical and mental health?

Nutritionists and scientists in related fields are constantly discovering ways that can improve your health and well-being. They are finding out that not only is your physical being adversely affected by poor nutrition but your mental capacity is as well. Recent scientific advances have demonstrated a direct relationship between mental retardation and severe malnutrition.

Should I be particularly careful about adequate nutrition at the time of conception, during my pregnancy, and during the first years of my baby's life?

Yes. Some of the most persuasive results of research in this field have been achieved by Dr. Bacon Chow and his associates at Johns Hopkins University School of Medicine in Baltimore, Maryland. The basic research has been done with rats, for it would hardly be practical or acceptable deliberately to deprive humans of necessary nutrients in order to prove a scientific theory. However, the results of Dr. Chow's research have led the investigation to Taiwan, where humans, who are deprived because of their natural diets, are being observed. Similar observations have been made by medical teams in Guatemala and other developing countries. The data support the contention that the physical and mental health of the child is dependent upon:

1. Adequate nutrition of the mother at the time of conception;
2. Adequate nutrition of the mother during the pregnancy; and
3. Adequate nutrition of the baby, especially during the first five formative years.

Dr. Chow and his associates, through exhaustive experimentation, have collected evidence which suggests that it is the quantity and quality of protein in the mother's diet which are the critical factors in determining the size of the offspring. Generally speaking, poor nutrition leads to smaller babies.

Are many children really malnourished?

Yes, and the sociological implications inherent in those children suffering from mental and physical retardation in our own country and in developing countries are enormous. According to the Pan-American Health Organization and its Advisory Committee on Medical Research, sixty to seventy per cent of all preschool children in developing countries, some four hundred million youngsters, are suffering from mild to moderate chronic forms of protein-calorie malnutrition. In other words, their diet does not include enough calories nor enough protein.

Now, if the developing countries are to develop and to catch up with twentieth-century technology, they must have a population capable of learning the necessary skills, and that demands mental as well as physical fitness.

Can severe malnutrition affect the personality of children?

Yes. In Mexico, Drs. Gomez and Robles have demonstrated that different forms of malnutrition altered personalities and behavior in children. In Venezuela, Dr. G. Barrera Moncada observed children with kwashiorkor and marasmus (severe diseases of malnutrition caused by starvation). They observed the children after their recovery, and then seven years later, and found that performance in all areas tested was poorer than among comparable children of the same genetic origin who had not suffered malnutrition.

How does a diet that is just plain poor affect the mental performance of children?

In South Africa, Drs. M. B. Stoch and P. M. Smythe observed two groups of children who belonged to contrasting social classes. One group had been fed a poor diet, the other a more adequate diet. During the seven-year study, Drs. Stoch and Smythe, using standardized tests, found marked differences in the mental performance of the two groups of children. The performance of the poorly nourished children was definitely inferior to that of their better-nourished peers.

Although many factors, such as social attitudes, cultural background, hereditary influences, general environment, and quality of diet contribute to the mental and physical growth of a child, there appears to be a correlation between poor performance in school, for example, and poor nutrition at home.

Can one be undernourished without going around hungry?

Because animal protein, that is milk, meat, eggs, butter, etc., is a relatively expensive item in a family food budget, it is not surprising that youngsters in our poverty areas, rural and urban, are going to suffer from protein deficiency. Many of these families can't afford enough protein. For example, they fill up on the cheaper foods, such as spaghetti and other pastas, rice, beans, bread, cereals, etc. Even though a child may not go hungry, he may well be undernourished.

Is malnutrition also a problem among the affluent?

Perhaps surprisingly, even the affluent, sophisticated urban-ite may also suffer from protein-calorie malnutrition. For example, there is the active, suburban housewife-community worker who grabs a glass of orange juice and a cup of coffee before dashing out to the 9:00 A.M. community-fund meeting, gulps down a sandwich and more coffee for lunch, spends the afternoon chauffeuring children, feeds them (quite possibly a well-balanced meal), and then meets her commuter husband. Before dinner, the exhausted wife and the equally tired business executive proceed to have one or two drinks or more with cheese and crackers, nuts, or other filling snacks to take off the cutting edge of the drink. By the time the pair sit down to dinner, their appetites have been blunted by the snacks, they experience a letdown feeling, and they probably pick at their dinner. Then there is the less active person who, perhaps because of boredom, finds time heavy on his hands once the children have grown and left home and who sits glued to the television set while stuffing his face with potato chips, nuts, etc. This kind of indolence and poor nutrition causes not only lack of energy but also obesity which, in turn, puts more burden on the already tired body; the result is a truly vicious circle.

Should I take a vitamin each day?

Malnutrition takes many forms. Since the discovery of vita-mins, particularly in the 1920's and 1930's, there was a great furor and hoopla about the necessity for adequate vitamin consumption since many diseases, such as pellagra, beriberi, rickets, etc., were found to be caused by lack of vitamins in the human diet. In the days and years which followed the early research into the properties and values of various vita-mins, widespread publicity in the lay press was given to the importance of these vital elements of the daily diet.

Since the general popularity of the fad diet has infused our overweight society, it would appear that most of what the public learned and took seriously a generation ago has become watered down in many minds. Nevertheless, the fact remains that vitamins are an integral part of any balanced diet, some vitamins obviously playing a more important role than others. But we repeat: it is not for the layman to decide which vitamins he does or does not need to supplement his daily diet. This decision is solely in the province of the physician. Indiscriminate use of vitamin pills can be not only costly but dangerous.

I have trouble seeing at night; could I have Vitamin A deficiency?

One of the most alarming incidences of vitamin deficiency has been documented in Canada: this is a lack of reserves of Vitamin A. According to Dr. T. Keith Murray, Chief of the Nutrition Research Division of the Canadian Food and Drug Directorate in Ottawa, Canada, there is a "shocking incidence of Vitamin A deficiency among Canadians," and, Dr. Murray continues, "I see no reason why the same would not be as likely to occur in the United States as well."

Vitamin A, which is essential to prevent night blindness, infertility, poor skin conditions, resistance to infection, and poor vision, is stored in fatty tissues of the body because it is soluble in fat. The liver is a particularly fatty organ, and it is here that more than ninety per cent of our Vitamin A reserves are stored.

In order for Dr. Murray and his researchers to study the levels of Vitamin A in humans, biopsies, or sections of human liver were taken of Canadians across the country during autopsies. These pieces of human livers from persons who had died were studied so that the amount of Vitamin A could be determined. The cadavers ranged from the stillborn to those ninety-two years of age, although most of the livers examined were of people over fifty-one years old. The causes of death were accidental, cancer, heart and coronary disease, respiratory disease, and other, less widespread, diseases. Of

the first one hundred liver specimens studied, eight showed
no detectable Vitamin A at all. Over thirty per cent of the
specimens showed alarmingly low levels of Vitamin A. Dr.
Murray reported to the Western Hemisphere Nutrition Con-
gress in 1968 that: "Since over ninety per cent of the body's
Vitamin A is stored in the liver, it is clear that a high proportion of Canadians were in unsatisfactory Vitamin A status
at the time of their death."

He went on to say: "It is hard to blame diet alone. Even
allowing for wastage, cooking losses, and uneven distribution,
it does not seem likely that so many of our population do
not get enough Vitamin A to maintain their reserves."

*Could environmental pollution, drugs, pesticides, and food
additives cause me to have a vitamin deficiency?*

If the average diet is sufficient in Vitamin A (in other
words, if most of us eat enough Vitamin A), what happens
to it after we eat it? Since the world is more aware than
ever of environmental problems, and of the possible dangers
of pesticides, drugs, and food additives, it is of particular
importance to pay attention to what Dr. Murray believes is
a possible cause of Vitamin A deficiency.

He suspects that some of the manufactured additives to
our food and environment are cutting down our ability to
use efficiently the Vitamin A we eat; or we may, in some
instances, be burning it up too fast.

Other investigators besides Dr. Murray have shown that
beef cattle fed forage from a field sprayed with DDT had
significantly reduced stores of Vitamin A in the liver, compared to steers fed from unsprayed forage. It has also been
shown that rats suffer from lack of Vitamin A when fed food
treated with DDT.

Although Dr. Murray has not been able definitely to determine the reasons for Vitamin A deficiencies in Canada, he
believes that it is possible that the deficiency may be due to
". . . an as yet unrecognized combination of diet and envi-

ronmental factors that are responsible for the low level of Vitamin A storage in the autopsy specimens."

Are most American women getting an adequate amount of iron in their diet?

Vitamin A is not the only nutritional deficiency found in North Americans; for example, most of us are familiar with radio and television commercials which warn about "iron-poor blood" and "iron-deficiency anemia"; and lately, the advertising men have been drumming home the message that women have a greater need for iron than men throughout most of their lives. Although the presentation of the advertising may smack of the typical hard sell, it is not idle talk. There is definite evidence to show that Americans, particularly women and teen-age girls, are not getting enough iron in their diets. According to Dr. Hilda S. White, Associate Professor of Home Economics, of Northwestern University, Evanston, Illinois, the recommended dietary allowance of iron for women and children is eighteen milligrams per day. Dr. White says that women today take into their systems an average of less than ten milligrams a day. Government nutritionists report that "Iron deficiency is almost certainly the most prevalent nutritional disorder among children in the United States."

If a girl is deprived of iron, it is easy to see why she may become anemic by the time she reaches adolescence and begins her menstrual cycle; iron is an essential for producing healthy blood. One reason for the "back to mother's milk" campaign among pediatricians is that mother's milk is two hundred and fifty per cent richer in iron than cow's milk. Of course, it is true today that a child who is not breast-fed is not put on a diet of plain cow's milk, but is given a formula which has been highly fortified with essential nutrients, including iron.

If you are to feel well, the importance of adequate iron in the diet cannot be overestimated. When lack of iron is sufficient to cause anemia, you feel constantly tired and will probably look it. To feel well, as well as to *be* well, and to present a picture of physical well-being, you must have healthy blood. In order to have that healthy blood, you must have a diet adequate in iron.

Is iron deficiency also a problem for the teen-ager who might not eat a well-balanced meal?

Rebellion among teen-agers takes many forms, as most parents and every person aware of today's sociological problems realize. The ways in which young people rebel run the gamut from mild disobedience to self-destruction through the use of drugs. There are teen-agers who rebel by employing another form of self-destruction, perhaps one not as critical as drug abuse, but equally disturbing, and occasionally, almost as difficult to treat.

A young girl of fifteen, E. S., was just such a youngster. Her rebellion against her parents through overeating had netted her a gain of eighty-one pounds over her ideal weight. Food was not only her pacifier but her "drug." She ate for taste, which satisfied a kind of sensual craving, and definitely not for nutrition. She was on a steady diet of pizza, hamburgers, and Coke. In addition to her excess weight, she had developed facial skin blemishes. Laboratory results showed that her poor nutrition had resulted in her becoming anemic. In short, her uncontrolled eating patterns had far from alleviated her adolescent emotional problems, but had, instead, multiplied them manyfold.

E. S. was placed on a well-balanced diet and given the required dosage of iron to combat her anemia. Her parents were told not to bug her about what she ate (constant friction about her eating patterns had only caused her to rebel by eating just what she shouldn't have). She lost eight pounds a month over a period of a year, and her facial blemishes and anemia cleared up. She has maintained her reduced weight for the past eighteen months.

What foods are high in iron?

Red meats, especially liver, green vegetables, whole wheat, egg yolk, carrots, and fruit.

I am pregnant and have a Vitamin B (folic acid) deficiency. Can I pass it on to my unborn child?

Recent medical research has pointed up another diet deficiency which has far-reaching implications. Dr. A. Leonard Luhby of New York Medical College, in a study of two hundred and fifty pregnant women, found that twenty-two per cent were deficient in folic acid, one of the B vitamins. Before one's bone marrow can produce normal red-blood cells, it must have a sufficient supply of folic acid. Dr. Luhby says that *pregnant women who do not have enough folic acid in their bodies can pass their deficiencies on to their unborn children.* This lack of enough folic acid in the mother may lead to retarded growth and birth defects in the child.

Dr. Luhby says: "Folic-acid deficiency in pregnant women could well constitute a public health problem of dimensions we had not originally recognized." Early detection by obstetricians and prenatal clinics can remedy the deficiency by adding proper amounts of folic acid to the pregnant woman's diet.

What foods should I eat to prevent a folic-acid deficiency?

You should eat liver, kidneys, mushrooms, yeast, and the deep-green leafy vegetables. Folic acid is lost rapidly from food stored at room temperature so care should be taken to use quickly or to refrigerate promptly. Raw vegetables will retain more folic acid than those that have been cooked.

Could I be deficient in zinc?

For some time, it has been suspected that a lack of zinc cuts down food absorption. Laboratory experiments have shown that animals fed diets deficient or totally lacking in zinc become emaciated. Animals have also exhibited retardation in body growth and hair growth when there is not enough zinc in the diet.

There is now evidence from researchers in Australia to enforce the suspicions about zinc deficiency in humans. Three doctors, according to the February, 1969 edition of *Medical World News*, reported in a detailed study two patients' dramatic improvement when zinc treatment was added to other therapy. One case was that of a seventy-one-year-old woman who, following abdominal surgery, developed extremely delicate skin resulting in skin ulcers or bad sores. After a week of zinc therapy, most of the skin sores were almost all healed, and healing of the surgical incision was greatly improved. In the second case, a seven-month-old boy was shown to be deficient in zinc. Zinc treatment produced marked general health improvement and weight gain in the infant.

What foods are rich in zinc?

Zinc may be obtained by eating lean meat, kidneys, liver, fruit, green leafy vegetables, and whole-grain cereals.

Could protein deficiency be causing me to have trouble with my hair?

We have previously discussed the seriousness of lack of protein in the human diet. Recently, nutrition scientists at the University of California at Berkeley have shown that the condition of a person's hair roots can show whether or not he is suffering from protein malnutrition. In addition to the condition of the hair roots being a symptom of protein malnutrition, it is apparently a cause of lack of hair color and a drying up or wasting away of hair-root bulbs. The researchers took eight healthy male volunteers and kept them in a hospital research ward for three months. The men, aged twenty-four to twenty-nine, were fed a liquid-formula diet three times a day. One group received seventy-five grams of

protein a day in the formula diet while the other group had
no protein at all. Each man in both groups received 2,800
calories a day. At the conclusion of the experiment, samples
of a hundred hairs were plucked from the back of each
subject's head and examined under a dissecting microscope.
The hair from the heads of the men who had been deprived
of protein showed less color and the root bulbs were
atrophied.

*I was told I was a Yo-Yo because I had a deficiency of mag-
nesium, which adversely affected my enzymes. Could this
be so?*

Yes, another mineral which is essential to good health is
magnesium. Until recently, magnesium deficiencies were not
given the respect which we now know they deserve.

Magnesium is important because it regulates vital processes
within cells; it affects the well-being of muscles, nerves, the
brain, the kidneys, the liver, and other organs. All these
organs normally contain a certain amount of magnesium.
When the magnesium content falls below certain levels, the
organs, quite naturally, do not function to capacity.

Dr. John Prutting, President of the Foundation for the
Advancement of Medical Knowledge, says:

> Magnesium is especially important as an activator of
> enzymes through which we use protein and vitamins.
> It also helps the utilization of potassium. Magnesium
> starts the chain reaction in the body to metabolize food.
> In fact, many of the nutrients we consume do us no
> good unless magnesium is present in the proper amount.
> For example, undernourished hospitalized patients
> given large doses of Vitamin B_1 and other vitamins by
> injection remained deficient in those same vitamins
> until magnesium was added to the injections; then the
> vitamin deficiencies cleared. Similarly, doctors working
> with children suffering protein-calorie malnutrition have
> noted that vitamins and minerals do not help these
> children without the addition of magnesium.

What are the signs and symptoms of magnesium deficiency?

Constipation, mental fatigue, feelings of being unable to cope with unusual problems, irritability, depression, anxiety, muscle cramps, palpitation, accelerated heart beat, and irregular heart beat are some of the most frequently seen signs and symptoms.

What causes magnesium deficiency?

One surprising cause is too much high-calcium food and excess protein. Calcium, when excessive, competes with magnesium, and will be absorbed in preference to it. In regard to protein, the more protein food you eat, the more magnesium you need. Too much sugar in the diet can also lower magnesium absorption. Excessive use of alcohol can deplete magnesium stores. Therefore, watch out for "fad diets" that emphasize the extreme use of any of these foods. Dr. Prutting says that "People who habitually start the evening meal with Martinis, a cheese appetizer, and go on to steak or hamburger with potatoes and dessert lower their magnesium level dangerously."

A word of caution to persons habitually using diuretics to control fluid retention: along with the water loss there is also a loss of magnesium.

I am on a high-protein diet; what foods will protect me from becoming magnesium deficient?

The best food sources of magnesium are nuts (especially almonds) and seeds—sunflower, sesame, caraway, and pumpkin. Wheat germ, oatmeal, corn, and cornmeal are excellent. High on the list of magnesium-rich foods is peanut butter, so there is obviously an important nutritional value in the American children's favorite peanut butter and jelly sandwich. Fresh green vegetables, when cooked in small amounts of water, also yield valuable amounts of magnesium.

As with everything else, moderation and balance in the

diet is the keynote to good nutrition. For dynamic equilibrium, proper nutrition is the answer.

Are there health hazards in being overweight, as there are health hazards in being undernourished?

Yes, as the following chapter will show.

12

Health Hazards of Obesity

Should I be concerned about being fat?

"So, I'm fat! So what? I'm just one of those people who were born to be fat. My mother and her mother were also fat. Anyway, I've tried dieting and it never works; so I've just decided to try and be happy though fat."

Does this imaginary monolog sound familiar? You probably all have heard similar statements, and perhaps some of you have made them.

So, you're too fat; so what? *So,* you may be endangering your health and indirectly cutting your life short. Look around: how many old *fat* people do you see? Not very many.

In this chapter the health hazards of obesity are given, as well as some of the reasons for concern over them. Each disease will be discussed in detail in individual chapters.

According to the United States Department of Health, "In fat patients who are otherwise in good health, the risk of developing major illnesses seems higher than in people of normal weight, but the magnitude of the risk cannot currently be specified because the existing data have too many epidemiologic defects [variables causing obesity]. . . ." "The hazards to health will vary from individual to individual and

must be viewed from the standpoint of the individual's total
health. . . ."

Will my being overweight cause my death?

Medical scientists concede that it is unlikely that overweight or obesity in itself causes death. Obesity contributes,
however, to many other conditions of ill health which do
cause death, and it highly complicates many other diseases
which could be more successfully managed if you were of
desirable weight.

*Does the degree of my fatness determine how bad my health
problems may be?*

As early as 1954, it was found by medical researchers that
in obese persons there were at least transitory abnormalities
of almost *every* body function. The discouraging facet of this
research is that the degree of obesity does not always seem
to affect the seriousness of the trouble. Some excessively
fat persons may have only mild problems, while others only
slightly overweight may have a major difficulty. It hardly
seems fair but it is a medical fact of life. Perhaps the obesity
is not the cause of the trouble, but it may be a coexistent
feature since certain disorders are seen so often in obese
patients that one is forced to infer that there may be a direct
relationship between the disease and the obesity.

When I gain weight I have trouble breathing. Why?

You have to breathe to live. Have you ever tried to walk
with a fifty-pound pack on your back? It's not easy, and
one reason for the difficulty is the extra load. For the obese
person, the process of breathing becomes more difficult because there is more weight on the chest wall. Then it takes
more work to supply enough oxygen to the blood so it, in
turn, can supply oxygen to the brain and the extra tissue.

In cases of gross obesity, the situation can become serious.
Breathing decreases, which results in less oxygen being taken

into the blood stream, and carbon dioxide builds up. When this happens, the person becomes sluggish and lethargic. However, it is possible in most cases to reverse the situation by weight reduction: if not, death can ultimately ensue.

Are there other dangerous complications from the lack of oxygen?

Yes, too much fat can cause another, worse complication due to a lack of enough oxygen in the blood of the arteries. When this happens, the number of red cells increases and, in turn, the danger of a thrombosis, or a blood clot, increases. The latter could possibly lead to heart attack, stroke, and death.

Can my extra weight cause heart disease or a heart attack?

Again, it must be emphasized that being too fat will not cause heart disease; at least, at present, there is no evidence which says it will. However, it is only reasonable to assume that too much weight puts an extra burden on the heart, and this cannot be good for the heart. After all, an ordinary two-door sedan which must pull a two-ton trailer up a hill time and again is going to wear out a lot faster than if it only had to pull a one-ton trailer up the hill.

Controlled scientific studies of men and women with both mild and serious heart conditions have shown that reduction in weight does help in the control of the disease and cuts down the frequency of heart attack.

What will the extra pounds do to my blood pressure?

In general, blood pressure tends to go up as your weight increases. This is not to say that five or ten pounds of overweight is likely to create a serious blood-pressure problem, but the greater the weight gain, the greater the risk of having high blood pressure. Several studies have been done to examine the relationship of weight to blood pressure and the results have shown that there appears to be a direct relationship because of an increased resistance of the blood vessels.

Mr. B. J. was sixty-five years old and twenty-two pounds overweight when he was first examined by me. He had carried this excess weight for the past six years.

Little by little, he had noticed that he became tired more easily and was not as efficient as he had been formerly in performing mental and physical tasks. He had a difficult time remembering events, especially those which had occurred recently. He told me he developed "heartburn" after each meal and frequently had pain in his chest and down his left arm.

During his physical examination, he was shown to have abnormal pulsations in his arms and legs plus high blood pressure. X rays showed considerable calcification of his main blood vessels and arteries. An electrocardiogram supported the diagnosis of a cardiovascular condition called angina pectoris.

B. J. was placed on six evenly spaced meals a day, and his salt intake was limited. The smaller, more frequent meals reduced the burden on the narrowed blood vessels and arteries to his heart. When food is digested, blood flow is increased; so obviously, three larger meals a day increase the work of the heart and the blood flow, more than if food is ingested more frequently and in smaller quantities. When the vessels and arteries are decreased in size for any reason, it is reasonable to alleviate the situation as best one can.

Within six months, B. J. had lost twenty of the excess twenty-two pounds and his angina pectoris symptoms had subsided. For the last fifteen months he has maintained his weight loss.

One study done by Dr. J. Stammler under the auspices of the University of Michigan School of Public Health illustrates the relationship between high blood pressure and overweight.

The researchers examined 746 men who worked for a Chicago utility company. Both weight- and blood-pressure measurements were taken over a period of twenty years. For this reason, some of the men were young adults when the study began.

The men who were overweight as young adults had higher blood pressures as older men than did their fellow workers who had been of a desirable weight or slightly underweight when they were young.

Most of the men in the Chicago study were slim when they were young, but the majority switched to the overweight group as they got older, and, by the time they reached so-called middle age, they were in the obese category.

The relatively small number of men who remained Slim Jims had the lowest incidence of high blood pressure. And it was found that the higher the weight gain, the higher the blood pressure. It worked out in almost direct proportion.

From the Chicago and other studies, the United States Department of Health has concluded that:

1. More hypertension (high blood pressure) exists among the obese than among the non-obese;
2. The obese person with high blood pressure experiences a greater risk of coronary heart disease and heart attacks than the non-obese person with high blood pressure;
3. Death rates for obese persons with high blood pressure are higher than those for persons who are only obese or for those with high blood pressure, without the complicating obesity.

Does obesity affect diseases other than those primarily associated with the heart and arteries?

Yes, there also appears to be a definite relationship between maturity-onset diabetes and obesity. It is particularly important for a person with a history of diabetes in his family to keep his weight at desirable levels.

There are conflicting theories about the relation of weight

gain to maturity-onset diabetes. There is one school of thought which adheres to the belief that the onset of active diabetes is triggered by excessive weight. Still another group of researchers believes that it is the manifestation of the diabetes which, in fact, causes the weight gain. More complete knowledge about these theories and the chemical action of insulin will be discussed in Chapter 17.

Suffice it to say that maturity-onset diabetes is usually accompanied by serious weight gain as in the case of H. R., a sixty-three-year-old man who, until recently, had maintained his normal weight. Three weeks prior to his being examined by me, he had been involved in an automobile accident, and in that short time had gained twenty-five pounds.

This gentleman complained of excessive fatigue and pain in his weight-bearing joints. He also reported being oversensitive to heat.

Laboratory data showed that his glucose, or sugar metabolism was abnormal and that he was, in fact, a victim of early diabetes. The accident had triggered an emotional trauma which led to bad eating habits that, combined with his enforced physical inactivity, had resulted in his weight gain. He was placed on a special diet and given oral anti-diabetic medication. Within three months, symptoms of fatigue, pain in his joints, and intolerance to heat had subsided, and his weight had returned to normal. He has been symptom-free, with a normal blood-sugar reading for the past year.

Will exercise help reduce my "spare tire"?

It is more common than not, for persons of middle age, say forty to fifty, to put on weight, especially around the middle. You may, like many, attribute the added fat to your age and refer to it as the "middle-aged spread." You may consider the phenomenon natural and impossible to do anything about.

You may say to your physician when he admonishes you

to take off the excess poundage, "But, doctor, I eat just the same as I always have but I keep gaining." What you don't realize is that although you may not have changed your eating habits, you probably have decreased your physical activity. In that case, you are not burning calories as you did before, and the result is that the body stores the excess calories as fat. The result is overweight and even obesity. Exercise can reduce this "spare tire."

Are there any special hazards if I am obese and pregnant?

If you are of childbearing age, it is extremely important that you do not become obese. Obesity can lead to serious complications during pregnancy. Stillbirths occur more frequently when the mother is too fat; delivery is complicated and, when anesthesia is needed, the hazard is further increased, as it is in any surgery requiring general anesthesia. Other complications of a serious nature include high blood pressure, serious water retention, and kidney failure.

After a pregnancy can my body chemistry so change as to make weight loss almost impossible?

It is not at all uncommon to hear of young women who have always had slim, trim figures suddenly losing their cherished slimness after their first pregnancy. There are various causes for this phenomenon, and sometimes it is due to subtle changes in your body chemistry, as demonstrated by the case of Mrs. J. C., a twenty-six-year-old mother.

Like many young mothers, she had had an ideal figure prior to her first pregnancy, but soon after began steadily to gain weight. At the time I examined her, she was sixty-seven pounds overweight.

Mrs. J. C. complained of abnormal breathing on exertion, such as climbing stairs. Her swollen feet were causing her considerable discomfort, and she had been told she suffered from flat feet. During this time, she had developed arthritis of the knees and lower back. Of course, all these symptoms—common in cases of obesity—were greatly aggravated by her excessive body weight.

After a thorough physical examination and laboratory tests, it was shown that she was hypothyroid and was lacking in a specific thyroid hormone called T-4. Recent scientific knowledge now enables physicians to determine through laboratory testing which specific hormone of the thyroid gland is lacking in the patient, so that replacement can be accomplished. In other words, until scientists were able to break down the thyroid gland into its component hormones, it was only possible to administer desiccated thyroid, containing all the thyroid hormones. The result of this was an increase, but not necessarily a correction, in the concentration of the hormone in which the patient was deficient. In addition, the patients were given, in effect, additional medication which they often did not need. For the past few years, it has been possible to determine exactly which hormone is needed by individual patients and to administer the required dosage.

After ten months of T-4 medication and a sensible diet, the patient achieved her ideal weight, regained her trim figure, and was no longer plagued by difficulty in breathing, foot trouble, or arthritic symptoms. For the past six and one-half years, she has maintained her weight and continues free of her former symptoms. It has been necessary, however, for her to continue her T-4 medication.

Occasionally, as in the case of Mrs. J. C., the thyroid gland ceases to be capable of producing one or more of the thyroid hormones. Not all the reasons for this are clear, but we do know of instances where thyroid hormone production has been reduced or totally stopped by excessive radiation, by consumption of shellfish contaminated by radioactive pollutants, and by virus infections.

Will my being overweight affect my sex life?

There is another serious side effect of obesity which cannot help but be important in the over-all physical- and mental-health picture. If you are a grossly obese person you will find your sex drive diminishing. You just aren't as interested; this can create a problem, especially if your marriage partner is thin! The lack of sexual response on the part of one partner in a marriage can be devastating to the relationship. Then too, obese women frequently develop menstrual irregularity, and during childbearing years, this can be nerve-racking—particularly to the woman who has already borne her family. The fear of pregnancy for the middle-aged woman is a real social and psychological problem, but when it is complicated by uncertainty from month to month, the result may be severely damaging. Add to this the factor of obesity, the lack of sex drive complicated by the inhibiting factor of fear of pregnancy, and you have a grave problem, not a minor one. This is not to imply that the fat girl's slim sisters never have menstrual difficulties, but it has been shown that the chances are greater for the obese woman.

Does obesity worsen arthritic pains? Would my losing weight help?

Yes, if you are arthritic and obese you are likely to suffer proportionately more than your thin counterpart. To date, we still know precious little about the causes and treatment of arthritis, but we do know, in part, what it is. In simple language, it is an inflammation, deformity, and stiffening of the joints, often causing considerable pain. As the joints stiffen and become more difficult and painful to move, any additional weight imposed on them naturally increases the pain. It is not uncommon, if you are seriously overweight and arthritic, to notice a difference in the amount of pain and in the ease of moving about once weight reduction is achieved. Losing weight won't cure arthritis of any kind, but it will lessen the discomfort in most instances.

Should I use a diet low in salt?

Cutting down on the salt in the diet will cut down on fluid retention, advisable where a person has any heart condition or is subject to abnormal retention of fluid. You should consult your doctor for the specifics.

What will a diet high in salt do?

In a diet high in salt, a person with a heart condition will most probably retain fluid and could end up with pulmonary edema—fluid in the lungs—which would necessitate immediate emergency treatment.

Can anything bad happen to me if I use diuretics?

Diuretics are chemical substances to rid the body of excessive fluids. There have been cases of ill-advised physicians prescribing the *constant* use of diuretics for patients with weight problems; and even worse, persons who self-administer diuretics. If used improperly, diuretics also deplete the body of other substances, particularly potassium. Potassium is essential to maintain life. If potassium is lost, blood pressure may drop, and eventually the heart will stop: a rather grim prospect. In addition, overuse of diuretics is also known to irritate the kidneys, even to the point of causing serious malfunction of these organs; this can be a very serious matter. Excessive use of diuretics can also cause diabetes.

If I am fat will I age faster?

Most persons do not realize that when their overweight turns into obesity, their physiology as well as their outward appearance changes. Our research team demonstrated this dramatically. In the study of twelve obese patients in their thirties, some as much as twice their normal weight, we found that their psychophysiological profile was startlingly like that of healthy seventy-one-year-old men who had been observed at the Gerontology Center of the National Institute of Health located at Baltimore City Hospital. Our report stated: "An average life expectancy of obese persons of this type is approximately fifteen years less than that of their normal age group. From the standpoint of these 'lost years,' obesity may be regarded as a form of premature aging."

Can a young fat man's heart show a decrease in function like that of an old thin man?

Yes, and when he loses his excess weight his heart will return to its normal functioning.

13

Heart Disease and the Overweight Body

If I am overweight, does this increase the chances that I will have a heart attack?

The answer must be a *qualified* "yes," because in certain persons, obesity appears to have little effect. But it is safe to say that overweight and obesity can contribute greatly to the likelihood of heart attacks.

Dr. Herman K. Hellerstein, a nationally known cardiologist from Case Western Reserve University School of Medicine, explains it this way· "Obesity, by itself, from a standpoint of cardiovascular disease [disease associated with the heart and circulatory system], is important." He further explains that the important correlation between obesity and heart disease is greatest for that unfortunate person who also suffers from high blood pressure and/or diabetes. According to Dr. Hellerstein:

> Many people who become obese in America are obese because the food they eat is predominantly high in animal fat and/or refined sugars. At the same time, the number of calories they actually burn up each day is very low. Life in America today requires increasingly less physical activity. . . . Now, on the other hand, in other parts of the world there are people who eat starchy diets of rice and pasta, and who suffer from the same overweightness but they don't tend to have the same diseases as Americans because their food is not

high in saturated animal fat such as our good, juicy, marbled steaks.

Now, if a person of normal weight becomes overweight and finally obese and is a potential candidate for heart disease, then excessive fatty substances can lead to clogging of his arteries. In some instances obesity can lead to the development of high blood pressure which, in turn, has a big influence upon the premature acceleration of the clogging of the arteries.

Why are women more concerned about being overweight than men?

Dr. Hellerstein explained: "One of the most important things to emphasize is the concept of 'peer susceptibility.' Women, for example, are less overweight today than they were twenty years ago. A teen-age girl is more apt to have weight control by diet, not for health reasons, but for body image. So, the peer concept is very important in keeping your weight down."

If my wife and I are both overweight to the same degree, am I more susceptible to heart disease than she?

Yes. Statistics show that you are far more likely than she is to suffer from a heart attack. As Dr. Hellerstein stated: "My personal interest in overweightness and obesity is predominantly in the male, because the male is oversusceptible to heart disease before the age of fifty, to premature development of coronary disease, hardening of the arteries, etc."

Will losing weight make me more physically fit?

Dr. Hellerstein believes strongly in the importance of exercise not only for weight control but for general physical fitness. He says:

I think it is very important to point out that a person who loses weight does not automatically become more physically fit. In our studies, we found that in measuring the maximum amount of oxygen that the person is

capable of using, the person who lost weight and did
not also train became a *less fat* person who was sloppy
and unfit.

Previously, they were *fat*, sloppy, and unfit persons.
When one loses fat, one should also gain muscle. I
don't think this is emphasized enough.

*Can my keeping more physically fit help to prevent a heart
attack; or at least slow up the process of hardening of the
arteries?*

Most of you are aware that in many parts of the country,
extensive studies are constantly being carried out to determine the effect of diet, obesity, smoking, exercise, etc., on
middle-aged populations, in the hope that more knowledge
will help to reduce the incidence of coronary and other kinds
of heart disease, particularly in men. One interesting study
is now in its tenth year at the Jewish Community Center in
Cleveland, Ohio. The study is under the direction of Dr.
Hellerstein. The group consists of 656 middle-aged men of
whom 254 have coronary artery disease. Dr. Hellerstein says:

> We have been interested in studying the effects of
> physical fitness and training upon the prevention of cor-
> onary artery disease in one group and, secondly, upon
> the modification or easing of the process of hardening
> of the arteries in people who have already had a heart
> attack.
> We have the patients keep a diary of what they eat
> for seven days or longer so that we have an idea of how
> they eat. In addition to the dietary evaluation, we
> measure the amount of body fat. We take samples of
> body fat so that we know the composition of the fat.
> We have them wear a tape recorder which records their
> heart rate and we take an electrocardiogram during
> forty-eight hours of continuous daily living and sleeping.
> This lets us know how many heart beats there are for
> energy expenditure. In addition, each person is given a
> battery of psychological tests.
> We then prescribe for them a program of physical

activity using approximately 400 calories an hour, three times a week. Of course, 400 calories an hour, one or three times a week, is not prescribed at the very beginning because very few people could do it. The physical exercise is begun gradually, with a goal of 1,200 calories a week.

These people average 10 to 17 percent overweight initially and as they begin the exercise program, there is a significant loss of weight, but only statistically significant, for it amounted to about six or seven pounds. However, the important thing was that many people changed their body form. The belly that was protuberant, the cheeks and jowls that were full became thinner and the muscles increased. So the weight itself is a very poor index; but they decreased body fat as indicated by changes of fat folds. The beneficial effects of this change in body form and diet and activity was that they did lose weight while they changed their body form. They could safely take more exercise; they became more physically fit, and, up to the present time—and this is most important of all—the mortality (death) rate has been reduced about 50 percent and this is by patients who have coronary artery disease.

How does a high cholesterol level contribute to a heart attack?

Most of you are aware of a substance called cholesterol which, when you eat too much of certain foods, such as eggs, forms deposits on the insides of blood vessels. When this happens, the passageway through which the blood cells pass gradually becomes narrowed. Sometimes the blood vessels are narrowed so severely that the blood gets stuck and forms a clot or a cluster which, in turn, blocks the flow of blood completely. When this happens in a coronary artery carrying blood to the heart, a heart attack occurs.

A certain amount of cholesterol is produced by the body itself and is referred to as endogenous cholesterol. Exogenous cholesterol is that which is contained in the foods we eat.

For this reason, persons who are found to have a high cholesterol count are usually advised by their physicians to cut down on saturated fats, such as those from meat, butter, egg yolk, etc. Cholesterol level in the blood does tend to increase with age, but prolonged studies have shown that there are critical levels that may spell danger.

One such study has been carried on over a period of some twenty years in Framingham, Massachusetts. During this time, more than five thousand men and women have been under close medical observation. Results of the study showed that among the men under forty-four years of age, those who had a cholesterol count of more than 265 ran a five times greater risk of heart attack than those with a count consistently under 220.

Could my cholesterol level remain high even though I eat foods low in cholesterol?

Most researchers will agree that too much cholesterol in the blood is dangerous, but not all experts agree that a change in diet will significantly improve the situation. It is fairly certain that in some instances a diet of foods high in cholesterol will increase the cholesterol in the blood, but it is not certain that once the cholesterol level has increased, it can be appreciably lowered by less cholesterol in the diet; however, and this is important, it *will* lower the cholesterol *somewhat* and it *will not* compound the problem by *increasing* cholesterol levels. Your doctor can best counsel you about this.

Does any one food contribute more to a high cholesterol level than another?

Probably the one which contributes most to the high cholesterol level in American diet is the egg. Dr. George V. Mann, a professor at Vanderbilt University School of Medicine in Nashville, Tennessee, says that most American men eat the equivalent of three eggs a day. This is partly because eggs are such a built-in part of the American breakfast and because egg yolk is so widely used, especially in the baking industry. One egg yolk contains 250 milligrams of cholesterol, so if you eat—in one form or another—four eggs a day, you're taking in one whole gram of cholesterol. Almost anyone taking in that much cholesterol a day is bound to get a rise in the amount of cholesterol in the blood and this could prove dangerous, especially for the more or less sedentary person.

What is the significance of unsaturated as against saturated fat in the diet?

Among those who raise questions about the importance of unsaturated fat in the diet is Dr. Mann, who participated in an intriguing study of the Masai tribe of East Africa. The Masai subsist largely on a diet of milk and meat. From the age of fourteen, they are bound by tribal tradition to eat a diet consisting of milk and meat and no vegetables for the next 20 years—a diet high in saturated fats.

In one study of two hundred Masai men, it was found that practically no high blood pressure was observed and electrocardiogram studies showed very little arteriosclerotic heart disease, that is, hardening of the arteries.

In a case study of four hundred Masai men and some additional women and children during a four-week period in 1962, some fascinating facts were produced. Despite the Masai high-fat diet, the amount of cholesterol in the blood is low and there is practically no incidence of coronary heart disease. At first glance, this evidence would tend to prove that diet is not related to coronary heart disease. However, there are other factors which may or may not explain this apparent contradiction.

In a report published in the *Journal of Atherosclerosis Research* in 1964, the researchers, including Dr. Mann, say:

While the Masai men do not have clinical cardiovascular disease of the atherosclerotic (narrowing of the arteries and blood vessels due to fatty deposits) type, there is no autopsy data to confirm their anatomical situation. One might consider two possibilities. Either such a diet does not in fact contribute to those consequences or the Masai have some other protecting mechanism which allows them to eat these foods with immunity. One possibility for the latter might be a large amount of exercise. We have shown that strenuous exercise prevents the hypercholesterolemic (high cholesterol) effects of overeating and Golding has shown the influence of exercise in lowering serum cholesterol.

One might argue that the Masai are relatively freer of emotional and competitive stresses which, some believe, contribute to hypercholesterolemia and cardiovascular disease. More than most primitive people, the Masai find subsistence easy, labor light. Competition is negligible and, some might think, frustrations limited. They have few responsibilities and a quite different attitude toward the world and people about them than do most of us. It remains to be demonstrated whether this attitude toward life and its complexities is the nature of their immunity.

Can I be checked for other factors that may increase my chances of heart attack?

Dr. Donald S. Frederickson, Director of Intramural Research at the National Institutes of Health, National Heart and Lung Institute, and Dr. Robert I. Levy, Chief of the Clinical Service, have come up with some new and important findings.

First of all, they have devised a simple, inexpensive blood test which identifies five types of heredity-caused blood-fat abnormalities that increase the risk of coronary heart disease one hundred times or more. Drs. Frederickson and Levy have also found that not only is a high cholesterol count dangerous but an abnormal amount of triglycerides (fatty substances) in the blood is also dangerous. They have also shown that your genes (about which you can do nothing) are a factor in determining your chances for a heart attack, that there are five different types of blood-fat abnormalities which can be identified, and that special diet and medication can reduce the risk of heart attack.

It is now possible for a physician to have your triglyceride levels checked and to determine into which of the five categories you fall. For each type, there is a recommended diet which the physician may obtain from the National Institutes of Health. Of course, high triglyceride and cholesterol counts are not the only factors which increase the risk of heart attacks. Other complications, such as excessive overweight, inordinate stress, diabetes, high blood pressure and excessive smoking also contribute.

If I stop smoking will my heart behave as if I had never smoked?

Another important risk factor in heart disease is smoking. Dr. Mann says:

> When you stop smoking cigarettes, you immediately begin to behave (physiologically) as though you had always been a nonsmoker. Now, that's not true for the lungs. If you've smoked for 20 years, you have accumulated cancer risk and to stop smoking doesn't wipe the slate clean. You've had it. It's there. But, it seems that it does for coronary. That is, the week after you stop smoking, you begin thereafter to act like you had never smoked, physiologically speaking.

What are the two most important things I can do to prevent a heart attack?

Whichever view experts take regarding the relationship of high-fat diets to heart disease, most agree that exercise and the relief of undue stress are very important factors in the prevention of heart attack.

Experiments have shown that exercise improves carbohydrate metabolism and cuts down cholesterol deposits in your blood. Although body *weight* may not change significantly through a daily exercise program, in the course of three to six months the body *fat* will diminish. In turn, muscle tissue increases, resulting in a dramatic change in body composition.

A word of caution about exercise. Exercise programs, like diets, for persons who have lived a more or less sedentary existence, should be carried out under medical supervision. It certainly is not wise for a forty-year-old man with a nine to five desk job to suddenly start jogging a mile every day. Only his physician can properly advise him as to how and what to do. He may have been a great athlete in college, but if he hasn't done much more than push a lawn mower once in a while for the past twenty years, moderation and medical advice are the watchwords for him. The same advice applies to the middle-aged woman who no longer burns up countless calories caring for a family of young, active children. However, there are ways to balance your calorie intake with your degree of activity.

The following charts can give you a good idea of what kind of time and energy are involved in burning up some of the foods you eat. You can choose how to go about it. If, simultaneously, you are going to join a diet club, let's talk about it first.

Amount of Exercise Needed to Burn Up Certain Foods

Food	Calories	Running	Tennis (Singles)	Swimming	Riding Bicycle	Walking	Reclining
				Minutes of Activity			
Apple, large	101	5	8	9	12	19	78
Bacon, 2 strips	96	5	8	9	12	18	74
Banana, small	88	4	7	8	11	17	68
Beans, green, 1 cup	27	1	1	2	3	5	21
Beer, 1 glass	114	6	9	10	14	22	88
Bread and butter	78	4	6	7	10	15	60
Cake, 2 layer, 1/12	356	18	31	32	43	68	274
Carbonated beverage, 1 glass	106	5	8	9	13	20	82
Carrot, raw	42	2	3	4	5	8	32
Cereal, dry, ½ cup, with milk, sugar	200	10	17	18	24	38	154
Cheese, cottage, 1 tbsp.	27	1	1	2	3	5	21
Cheese, Cheddar, 1 oz.	111	6	9	10	14	21	85
Chicken, fried, ½ breast	232	12	20	21	28	45	178
Chicken, TV dinner	542	28	47	48	66	104	417
Cookie, plain	15	1	1	1	2	3	12
Cookie, chocolate chip	51	3	4	5	6	10	39
Doughnut	151	8	12	13	18	29	116
Egg, fried	110	6	9	10	13	21	85
Egg, boiled	77	4	6	7	9	15	59
French dressing, 1 tbsp.	59	3	4	5	7	11	45
Halibut steak, ¼ lb.	205	11	17	18	25	39	158
Ham, 2 slices	167	9	14	15	20	32	128
Ice Cream, 1/6 qt.	193	10	16	17	24	37	148
Ice Cream Soda	255	13	22	23	31	49	196
Ice Milk, 1/6 qt.	144	7	12	13	18	28	111
Gelatin, with cream	117	6	9	10	14	23	90
Malted milk shake	502	26	44	45	61	97	386
Mayonnaise, 1 tbsp.	92	5	7	8	11	18	71
Milk, 1 glass	166	9	14	15	20	32	128
Milk, skim, 1 glass	81	4	6	7	10	16	62
Milk shake	421	22	37	38	51	81	324
Orange, medium	68	4	5	6	8	13	52
Orange juice, 1 glass	120	6	10	11	15	23	92
Pancake with syrup	124	6	10	11	15	24	95
Peach, medium	46	2	3	4	6	9	35
Peas, green, ½ cup	56	3	4	5	7	11	43
Pie, apple, 1/6	377	19	33	34	46	73	290

Amount of Exercise Needed to Burn Up Certain Foods (Cont.)

Minutes of Activity

Food	Calories	Running	Tennis (Singles)	Swimming	Riding Bicycle	Walking	Reclining
Pie, raisin, 1/6	437	23	38	39	53	84	336
Pizza, cheese, 1/8	180	9	15	16	22	35	138
Pork chop, loin	314	16	27	28	38	60	242
Potato chips, 1 serving	108	6	9	10	13	21	83
Sandwiches:							
Club	590	30	52	53	72	113	454
Hamburger	350	18	30	31	43	67	269
Roast Beef with gravy	430	22	37	38	52	83	331
Tuna fish salad	278	14	24	25	34	53	214
Sherbet, 1/6 qt.	177	9	15	16	22	34	136
Shrimp, French fried, 2 jumbo	180	9	15	16	22	35	138
Spaghetti, 1 serving	396	20	34	35	48	76	305
Steak, T-bone, 3½ oz.	235	12	20	21	29	45	181
Strawberry shortcake	400	21	35	36	47	77	308

14

Diet Clubs

What has made diet clubs so popular?

Diet clubs in the United States may well be called a sign of the affluent times. What originally began with various groups of friends getting together to lend moral support to each other while trying to trim off excess weight has now become a multimillion-dollar business. The basic idea of a diet club is, in reality, a kind of group-therapy concept, which psychiatrists have used for many years to treat certain patients.

What attracts people to diet clubs?

There is no doubt about it, misery does love company, and for many persons, the *esprit de corps* of a group of his fellow men and women working together to achieve a common goal is a necessary crutch for success.

What precautions should I take in joining a diet club?

Anyone suffering with a serious weight problem should certainly never join a diet club without a thorough physical examination, including laboratory tests. There is always the possibility that the weight gain may be linked to a body malfunction. Stepping on the scale and having your blood pressure checked is definitely not enough.

Why not?

As I have emphasized previously, diets should be tailor-made to each individual, and this is perhaps the universal drawback of the club diet, which is generally handed out to all members. In some instances, these diets can do serious damage if your obesity is linked to an undetermined cause.

Let's consider K.D., a young man of twenty-seven. For as long as he could remember, he had been fat. From the time he had begun to be concerned about his weight and looks, he had dieted only to lose and regain. He calculated that he had probably lost and regained about seven hundred pounds during his lifetime!

When he was referred to me for diagnosis and evaluation he was already hospitalized. His breathing was labored, his blood pressure was too high, he had skin problems, and he had an array of digestive complaints.

He suffered from what I call plethoric obesity. In simple terms, his obesity was confined to his head, neck, throat, waist, and abdomen. His legs and arms were actually thin. He also had a buffalo hump on the back of his neck, and appeared moon-faced, with an excessive amount of fat in front of his ears. He actually looked as though he had the mumps.

Not long before being referred to me, he had joined a diet club—no doubt in desperation. There, he was told that there was nothing wrong with him except that he ate too much. He was given a high-protein diet and told to restrict his fluids. During the first week under club instruction, he lost twenty-two pounds. Most of the loss was of fluid. Shortly thereafter, he suddenly became dizzy and collapsed. At that point, he was hospitalized and brought to my attention.

A thorough examination showed that K.D. suffered from Cushing's Syndrome, or an overactive adrenal gland. He also proved to be severely dehydrated.

Once his lost fluid had been replaced, he was given proper

medication to correct the overactive adrenal gland. Then he was given a diet proper for *his* metabolism.

During the following thirteen months, K.D. lost eighty-seven pounds with a return to normal blood pressure. There is every reason to believe that he will continue to do well until he reaches his desired weight.

What can I learn from this experience?

This case demonstrates two important principles:

1. Extreme obesity or local distribution of fat is *uncommon* and suggests unusual origins. In this particular case, the adrenal gland was functioning abnormally and was corrected by proper medication; and,

2. The second basic principle is that *under no circumstance* should water intake be restricted during prolonged dieting since dehydration may ensue. *Excessive fluid* is effectively controlled, *not* by water restriction, but by salt restriction.

It might be pointed out that all natural foods contain a certain amount of salt, so restricting your table salt will not necessarily result in electrolyte depletion. But like all other diet restrictions, the amount of salt in your diet can be safely determined only by your physician.

The above case is, of course, an extreme example; however, it did happen, and unnecessarily. Cushing's Syndrome is not an everyday occurrence; had a competent physician examined the patient earlier, the symptoms would have been recognized, the condition treated, and the collapse of the patient avoided, thereby sparing the young man and his family considerable anxiety.

Are there safe diet clubs based on sound principles?

Not all diet club dieters end up like K.D. Like anything else, there are good, properly run diet clubs and there are those which are not. The key to a successful diet club is *proper supervision, both medically and nutritionally.*

Can you tell me what a well-run diet club should be like?

A diet club which was formed at the Johns Hopkins University School of Hygiene and Public Health is one which might well serve as a model for a well-organized, well-run club, under proper medical and nutritional supervision.

The T.O.W. (Take Off Weight) Club was formed under the supervision of Dr. Maria Simonson, an assistant professor in the Departments of Biochemistry and Psychiatry and Behavioral Sciences at the School, and Mrs. Gwen Campbell, an administrator at the School of Hygiene. Both women had had heart attacks and were well over their desired weight. Prompted by their own desire to lose weight and the desire to help others, they set up a *nonprofit club.* They enlisted the help of Dr. Bacon Chow, a biochemist and researcher in the field of nutrition, to aid them in nutrition problems. Facilities of the Johns Hopkins University were made available to club members with medical problems, including emotional disturbances.

Since the beginning of February, 1969, 311 persons have attended the group and 174 are still taking part in the program. This is how the T.O.W. Club works:

1. All members must be referred by an M.D. They must present to Dr. Simonson, the club lecturer, a medical history from the referring physician together with any recommendations he may have. The physician, in turn, is kept abreast of his patient's progress;

2. Once accepted, the member continues to eat exactly as always for one week. He keeps a detailed diary of the food he eats, the amount, the method of preparation (fried, baked, etc.), and at what time of day. This applies to *any* food whatsoever at any time during the one-week period. He also is asked to note what, if any,

emotional upsets he may have had during this period.

At the end of the week, a nutritionist and Dr. Simonson evaluate the member's food chart, taking into account the amount of food eaten, kind of food, time of eating, and emotional patterns;

3. Once the evaluation has been made, the member meets with Dr. Simonson and is placed on a prescribed diet. Certain cardinal rules are laid down:

   a. No meals may be skipped;

   b. No crash diets;

   c. No diet pills;

   d. No substitutions in the diet, unless ordered by his own physician (salt-free, low cholesterol, etc.);

4. Each person is given periodical, psychologically oriented questionnaires to fill out. These, again, are evaluated. Dr. Simonson's experience as a behavioral scientist and psychologist provides her with the insight into some of the emotional problems of the member. When the emotional problems are serious, the patient's own physician is consulted, and with his permission, the patient is referred to a hospital staff psychiatrist. In addition, if a member appears to adhere to the diet but is still unsuccessful in shedding pounds, after consultation again with his own physician, he is referred to the Department of Medicine at the hospital and an extremely thorough physical examination, including laboratory tests, is given. In several instances, physical problems which might easily go undetected in the ordinary yearly physical examination have been uncovered through this comprehensive testing.

A few simple rules are followed by each member. In order to be carried in the program, he must begin by attending at least eight consecutive sessions. At each weekly session, the member is weighed and there is a short pep talk by Dr. Simonson, together with a discussion of nutrition, health problems of overweight and obesity, dangers of poor nutrition, crash diets, drugs, new advances in weight control, and discussion of various forms of quackery.

Dr. Simonson emphasizes that there is no magic formula, that common sense is the real key. She explains the importance of relearning good eating habits, and at no time is a member made to feel guilty or a failure when he does not lose weight during the week. Even if he should gain, he is not scolded but rather there is an attempt made to find out what caused the backsliding.

In essence, the goals of the club are to help the members find the cause of their overweight problems, to show them, through lectures (occasionally with guest speakers), why people get fat, and how being fat affects the body, the mind, and the behavior. The members are also shown how emotional problems can, and do, affect eating habits.

Each member's problems are treated sympathetically and individually.

Membership dues are minimal, each member paying a registration fee of two dollars and a weekly dues of one dollar. In some instances, a clinic or physician refers a patient who is financially unable to pay even this small fee. In such instances, the member is given a "scholarship." To increase the motivation, various awards are given. Whatever money is left over is used for some charitable purpose. Each summer, a disadvantaged youngster is sent to summer camp.

Dr. Simonson, Dr. Chow, and Mrs. Campbell volunteer their professional services. Dr. Simonson explains:

> In our indoctrination sessions, we use a body model to show how the organs of the body function, basic principles of body chemistry, and how various body organs and functions are affected by improper eating habits. At each meeting, we emphasize the

dangers of a do-it-yourself plan. In some cases of
family stress, we hold conferences with family members and enlist their cooperation.

Our approach is basically the relearning of good
eating habits under competent medical supervision.
Results show that this approach does work in the
average overweight person who has no other dramatic illnesses or problems.

*There is no teaching hospital in our town. How else could
we have a "well-balanced-diet club"?*

Not everyone lives within reach of a university teaching
hospital, so it is, obviously, not possible to model every diet
club after Johns Hopkins' T.O.W. However, due to the growing concern of the medical profession for the welfare of the
obese patient, it seems feasible that any "diet club" could
retain the services of one or more physicians. Most schools in
which luncheons are served to students employ a qualified
dietitian who might volunteer to help work out well-balanced
diets. There are many alternatives which might be suggested.
Basically, the success of a diet club depends upon the leader-
ship and the motivation that each individual brings to the
project.

*How can my town protect its fat citizens from unscrupulous
diet clubs?*

Your city could follow the example of New York. Their
Department of Health considers the improperly run diet
clubs so dangerous that there is now a ruling in the Health
Code of New York City which requires organizers and lay
leaders of weight-reduction groups to register with the Health
Department.

The Department gives these reasons:

1. Overweight may be due not only to excess fat but may
   mask underlying disease, such as weight gain due to
   fluid retention in heart failure or hypothyroidism;

2. If overweight is indeed due to excess fat, the origin may be due to rare brain tumors or overactive adrenal glands;

3. Obesity can be related to profound psychological disturbances. If the obesity is removed without psychiatric treatment, aggravation of the basic disturbance may occur;

4. Every obese person should be screened for the diseases with which obesity may be associated, such as diabetes, high blood pressure, and coronary heart disease; and,

5. Not all obese persons should receive the same diet; for example, those with high levels of serum cholesterol should be placed on a low-calorie, serum-cholesterol-lowering diet.

Before joining any diet club, should I not know the answer to the question, "Could It Be My Glands?"

The next chapter will deal with this question.

15

Could It Be My Glands?

What is a gland?

The human body contains many glands. They are small saclike structures, each of which secretes various substances; some, called endocrine glands, secrete hormones. The glands I am concerned with in this chapter have an association with obesity. They are: the pituitary, which is located at the base of the brain; the thyroid, located in front of and on either side of the windpipe; the adrenals, two small glands, located above each kidney; the pancreas, lying behind the stomach; and the sex glands—the ovaries in females and the testes in males. The secretions of each of these glands are important in relation to each individual's body chemistry. Each of the secretions of all your glands performs a specific function for your body. Some of these functions relate to obesity.

Is there a special name for the study of glands that secrete hormones?

Yes, there is a branch of medicine which concerns itself primarily with this type of glandular function and is called Endocrinology. Advances in this field have been significant in the last twenty-five years, and knowledge increases rapidly. It is an extremely important field of research in the control of many faults in body chemistry and in the control of some diseases. The doctor who studies problems of the endocrine glands is called an endocrinologist.

What sort of problems can my endocrine glands cause?

In the past, physicians thought of endocrine-glandular problems in terms of severe disorders; obvious problems, such as hyperthyroidism (an overactive thyroid gland), and hypothyroidism (an underactive thyroid gland). Dr. William McK. Jefferies, a Cleveland endocrinologist and researcher, says: "Now we are realizing that there are very definite milder disorders. Sometimes our usual routine tests will not pick up these problems; it is only with some of the more sophisticated techniques that are becoming available today that we can pick up the abnormalities that were formerly missed by the other tests."

Do my glands help make me a unique individual?

No two people's metabolism is identical. Dr. Jefferies explains:

> Every person is a little different. It is extremely difficult to find two people who have exactly the same type of chemistry and this, apparently, is one of the reasons we are different, because we have slight differences in hormone production. We have been interested in the adrenal glands because the adrenals have the interesting function of enabling the body to adjust to changes in environment; this is probably saying, adjusting to stresses and strain.
>
> One of the things that we turned up rather early in our work was the fact that every person has his or her own characteristic pattern of excretion of substances resulting from the metabolism by adrenal hormones (metabolites). We were measuring, particularly, the adrenal hormones that have to do with protein building activity and the hormones that have to do with the carbohydrate regulating aspect. We found that every person has his or her own characteristic pattern of excre-

tion of these metabolites. We don't know for sure yet which is involved, but we suspect hormones are a factor in body build. For example, the difference between the very thin ectomorphic body type, the more rounded muscular mesomorph, and the plump endomorph is probably hormone related.

Which body type seems to have the most difficulty losing weight?

Dr. Jefferies says:

In the process of studying endomorphs, we found that they generally tended to have a higher excretion of metabolites of adrenal hormones than other body types. When given ACTH, which is the hormone which stimulates the adrenal gland, the endomorph's adrenal reaction was two or three times greater than that of other body types and the ectomorph the least of all. This led us to wonder whether this type of overresponse of the adrenals might in some way be related to the fact that these endomorphs generally tend to have the most difficulty with excessive weight.

Does too much of a hormone cause the obesity, or the other way around?

According to Dr. Jefferies:

It is tempting to say, "Well, because a specific person tends to have overresponsive adrenals, this explains his tendency to be a stress eater." When these people get under tension, they feel better when they eat because their system puts out more of an adrenal secretion called hydrocortisone which tends to increase the appetite. It could also explain the fact that these people seem to prefer carbohydrate foods rather than protein foods. On the other hand, you could turn it around and say, "This might not be the cause; it might be an effect." If a person is overweight, this may alter his body's metabolism so that the adrenals tend to be overresponsive. It is similar to the situation with regard to insulin, a hormone produced by the pancreas. Obese persons, as a group, tend to have overresponsive pancreas glands and produce excessive quantities of insulin. When they eat a certain amount of carbohydrate, they get a higher rise in insulin than a person who is not obese. But, here again, the question is, "Which is the cart and which is the horse?" in regard to the overweight and obese individual. It is extremely important to understand that when the obese person, through a normal well-balanced diet, returns to his ideal weight, his excretion and his production of adrenal hormone returns to normal.

How do abnormal gland functions lead to obesity?

In cases where obesity can be blamed on glandular problems, it is usually a case of one of three things: either the gland in question is secreting too much hormone, not enough hormone, or, in rarer cases, there may be a tumor of that particular gland.

S.S. was a twenty-year-old woman who was thirty-three pounds overweight when first seen in consultation by me. She had been of ideal weight until after she had had her tonsils out at the age of nine. Following her operation, she began to gain weight and, since then, had had a weight problem.

A thorough history, physical examination, and extensive laboratory tests finally produced the answer to her problem. After collecting a twenty-four-hour urine specimen, she was shown to have an abnormal amount of adrenal-gland hormones. She was placed on medication to correct this excessive adrenal-hormone secretion and given a special diet. Within three and one-half months, she had achieved her ideal weight and her adrenal gland function returned to normal.

She has maintained her weight for nine and one-half years and her adrenal-gland secretion has stayed normal without her having to continue the medication.

I feel bloated and gain weight just before my period. What can I do about this? Is it glandular?

Fluid retention in cases of obesity is a fairly common occurrence. Fluid retention in women ten days or so prior to the beginning of a menstrual period is also very common. Most women complain of feeling bloated just prior to their menstrual period. The weight shifts in any one given month may range from two or three pounds to as much as six to ten pounds. Very often, simply limiting the amount of salt in the diet will alleviate this problem and the discomfort caused by it. In some cases, however, the reasons for excessive fluid retention are more complex.

Could there be a glandular cause for fluid retention and excess weight gain before a period?

Yes, another case related to excessive hormone production by the adrenal gland was the case of Q.V., a thirty-two-year-old woman plagued by excessive weight shifts each month.

About ten days before the onset of Q. V.'s period, she generally gained five to ten pounds and felt very bloated and uncomfortable. After her period, her weight again fluctuated. She confessed that she was unable to enjoy food unless she used a large quantity of salt.

Q. V. had had an overweight problem ever since she began her menstrual periods eighteen years previously. When she was examined by me she was found to be forty-four pounds above her ideal weight. The weight gain occurring ten days before her period was caused by execss salt in the diet, which resulted in water retention. Laboratory tests revealed that Q. V. had an excessive amount of a hormone called aldosterone. This hormone is excreted by the adrenal glands and has the peculiar property of causing salt to be retained and potassium to be lost. To correct her hormone imbalance, she was given specific medication to reduce the effect of the excess-salt-retaining hormone. She was placed on a well-balanced, low-calorie diet, and within four months, she had lost her excess weight. For the past eighteen months, she has maintained her ideal weight of 103 pounds, with her aldosterone level returning to normal during this period.

What will happen to a boy if he does not produce enough sex hormones?

The adrenals are not the only glands which are related to the problems of overweight and obesity. Lack of sex hormones is also related to obesity. Take the case of T. K., a fifteen-year-old boy who was twenty-five pounds overweight and had excessively underdeveloped sexual organs. In addition, he had an eyesight problem which had led to a tentative diagnosis of a tumor of the pituitary gland. Brain surgery to remove the supposed tumor had been recommended.

After a thorough history was taken and a physical examination was performed during a diagnostic consultation visit, I noted that he had a significantly increased eating pattern. Laboratory tests showed that T. K.'s basic metabolic rate was low, as was his excretion of adrenal hormone. It was shown that the youth did not have a pituitary tumor but did have what is known as Fröhlich's Syndrome. This is a condition characterized by obesity and underdevelopment of the sexual organs due to a lack of sex hormones.

The boy was treated with chorionic gonadotropin, a hormone to stimulate sexual development, and his excessive appetite was curbed by having him drink an ice-cold, eight-ounce glass of water before each meal. He was also placed on a well-balanced diet.

At the end of three months, there was significant growth of the sex glands and by the end of the year they were normal. He also had reached his ideal weight.

He is now twenty-one years of age and normal in every respect. This is one clear-cut case of obesity being directly related to an endocrine or glandular disorder.

Will a hormone lack cause irregular menstrual periods, and how does this occur?

Yes, one of the more dramatic instances in recent history was the observation that many women in Nazi concentration camps, due to poor nutrition, had irregular menstrual cycles and, in some cases, ceased to menstruate at all. This can also happen in everyday society.

Let's take the case of E. O., a sixteen-year-old girl who was seventy-four pounds overweight when first examined by me. During a four-year period before her examination, she had gained and lost over one hundred pounds going from one crash diet to another. When she was not on a crash diet, she subsisted on a nutritionally poor diet of pizzas, hot dogs, and carbonated soft drinks.

During this four-year period, she had experienced irregular menstrual periods and complained of excessive fatigue and constipation.

Laboratory tests showed that her ovaries were not functioning properly, which explained her irregular and infrequent menstrual periods. Her treatment was a low-calorie, but nutritionally sound diet. She was given no medication whatsoever. Within fifteen months, she had lost the excess weight, her menstrual cycle returned to normal, and she has remained at her ideal weight of 125 pounds for over three years. This is a case where the menstrual problem was due to bad nutrition, and the *correct* and *only* required treatment was proper nutrition.

How will too little sex hormone affect a middle-aged woman following menopause?

Low production of sex hormone can also cause problems in middle-aged women. Only a competent physician can accurately diagnose such a physiological disorder and prescribe the correct treatment.

Mrs. C. G., forty-eight years of age, is a prime example of a complex obesity problem which entailed comprehensive examination in order properly to diagnose the cause and the proper treatment of her problem.

Since the onset of puberty, she had had weight problems. During a thirty-five-year period, she had gained and lost over one thousand five hundred pounds. Again, the Yo-Yo Syndrome. In Mrs. C. G.'s case, her excess weight or fat was confined to her breasts, abdomen, hips, and thighs. She complained about being unduly tired, having brittle nails, dry skin, and suffering black-and-blue marks.

During her yo-yo periods, she noticed that each time she lost weight, she regained the original amount plus an extra fifteen to twenty pounds.

Following her menopause, she consulted a physician who determined that her metabolic rate was low and put her on thyroid medication. This treatment appeared to help her for a few months, but soon she was just as tired and just as fat as ever. The thyroid dosage was increased, but it only made her jittery. The result was a drop in physical work and a drop in her sexual activity.

After a thorough history, physical examination, and laboratory work, I made the diagnosis of adipose genital dystrophy, a condition characterized by obesity of the breasts, abdomen, hips, and thighs. Her obesity was further aggravated by the fact that she had also developed a condition in which there was an abnormally low secretion of sex hormone. This latter condition caused the drop in her basal metabolic rate (BMR), and decreased sexual activity. Actually, her thyroid function had previously been normal. Her drop in BMR was due not to a thyroid malfunction but to her drop in sex-hormone secretion.

After determining the real cause of her obesity and sex problems, Mrs. C. G. was taken off thyroid medication and put on appropriate hormone replacement. Once her maladjustment was cleared up, her metabolic rate returned to normal. Within eighteen months, she achieved her ideal weight and has maintained it and been free of her former symptoms for seven years.

Another example of hormone deficiency which can be related to obesity is that of a female hormone known as estrogen.

Weight gain in women following menopause is not uncommon and very often is just accepted as a fact of life by the victim. In many cases, the condition goes untreated, and the unfortunate woman remains fat, and very often shows certain personality changes which are irritating not only to her but to her family and friends.

Mrs. B. W. was forty-three years old and was twenty-seven pounds over her ideal weight. Up until her menopause, she had had no trouble maintaining her proper weight and had lived her life full of vigor and with a cheerful disposition. During her menopause, she began to experience hot flashes, extreme fatigue, headaches, and spells of irritability. In addition, she began steadily to gain weight. Six months prior to being examined by me, she had developed pain in her lower back and above her knees.

Laboratory tests now showed that her body was not producing enough female hormones. This is a very common occurrence, and the condition is easily remedied by giving a patient a female-hormone medication known as estrogen. Medication of this kind can only be safely given after thorough laboratory tests and a complete physical examination. In instances where the patient has a history of breast tumors, for example, such treatment is not recommended. However, a competent physician will know whether female hormone replacement is advisable and how much should be prescribed for his patient.

In Mrs. B. W.'s case, there was no reason not to give the medication, so this was done. At the same time, she was restricted to a low-calorie diet, and within six months she had regained her ideal weight of 118 pounds. Her other symptoms vanished, and the pain from her osteoarthritis disappeared with the lessening of the weight on her back and her knee joints. Her disposition became sunny again, she regained her former vigor, and the frequent headaches ceased. She has maintained her ideal weight for four years. It has been necessary for her to continue her hormone medication. With proper treatment, her problems resulting from a scarcity of female hormones were completely reversed.

Whether I am fat or not, why should I suffer from menopause?

You shouldn't. If you are going through menopause and are experiencing hot flashes, headaches, irritability, and decreased sexual drive, you are low in female hormones and should see your doctor. He should be able to help you.

Do you consider obesity a disease or a sign of a disease?

There are many who consider obesity a disease. I do not agree with this assertion; rather, I believe that obesity is a sign of an underlying emotional disturbance, or a sign of a physiological disturbance, or both. Even if it is simply because you have slowed down your physical activity and have begun to eat too many calories, the resulting weight gain is still only a sign of the change in your behavior pattern. There are some forms of obesity, as you have seen in various case histories, that tell the doctor very clearly of a physiological or chemical imbalance.

C. K. was twenty-eight years old, had been losing and gaining weight for seven years, and at the time of her examination was thirty-six pounds over her ideal weight.

For the past six years, she had tried to become pregnant without success. Her menstrual periods were very irregular and she had developed an unusual amount of facial hair as well as hair between her breasts and below her navel. In addition, she had a bad case of acne and reported pain on both sides of her abdomen. Physical examination showed that both her ovaries were enlarged and that she also had multiple ovarian cysts. Her condition was diagnosed as Stein-Leventhal Syndrome, and surgery to reduce the size of her ovaries was recommended. Stein-Leventhal Syndrome is characterized by obesity, excessive body hair, high blood pressure, infertility, irregular menstrual periods, and multiple cysts.

The excess facial hair and the hair between her breasts and below the navel was due to a lack of female hormone and too much male hormone. Men's and women's glandular systems excrete both male and female hormones. When the proper balance is not maintained—for example, if a man's endocrine system is excreting too much female hormone—he may show some female characteristics; the converse is true with women. Following surgery to reduce the size of her ovaries, she was placed on a well-balanced, low-calorie diet. During the next seven months, Mrs. C. K. experienced tremendous physical improvement and lost her excess thirty-six pounds. Eighteen months later, she became pregnant and now has a normal five-year-old son.

Why might there be a lack of sex drive in a fat man?

It is common knowledge among physicians that there is a decided lack of sex drive in the extremely obese individual, particularly in men.

Sometimes this lack of sex drive in the obese male is due to more than just being fat. First of all, the obesity may well be due to a physiological cause, and the lack of sex drive, in some instances, can be blamed on a lack of male sex hormone.

I. W. was forty-nine years old and twenty-eight pounds over his ideal weight. Until two years before his diagnostic examination, he had felt well and had had no trouble keeping his weight under control; then he began, slowly but surely, to gain weight. For the past year, he had experienced a marked decrease in sex drive.

Laboratory tests showed him to be deficient in male sex hormone, testosterone. He was given medication to replace this hormone and put on a diet. Within four months, his weight had returned to normal and his sexual desire had returned. He has maintained his desired weight for eighteen months.

What effect can a very underactive thyroid gland have on an adult?

An underactive thyroid gland can and does cause excessive weight gain, but only about eight per cent of overweight and obese patients can blame a sluggish thyroid gland for causing their problems. Once in a while, physicians find patients whose overweight problem is caused not only by a slightly underactive thyroid but by a thyroid which is functioning at greatly reduced levels. When this occurs, the patient experiences more dramatic symptoms than a mere gain in weight. The case of I.S., a twenty-three-year-old woman, is a classic example of this situation.

Two years prior to her diagnostic examination she began to develop a general physical weakness and lethargy; her speech slowed down and her menstrual periods became irregular. In addition, her hair began to fall out. Six months before I examined her, she developed a remarkable sensitivity to cold and her perspiration decreased. Upon examination, she was found to have dry, coarse, pale skin; dry, brittle hair; sparse eyelashes and eyebrows; her tongue was enlarged; her lips swollen; her speech thick; and her thyroid gland noticeably enlarged. These symptoms are typical of low thyroid. Her metabolism was shown to be excessively low and her blood chemistry revealed a deficiency of thyroid hormone. In addition, she was twenty-four pounds over her ideal weight.

I. S. was diagnosed as a case of adult myxedema. This is a medical term for an advanced case of a deficiency of thyroid hormone. In such a situation, thyroid hormone is indeed the proper medication, and was given to this patient, along with a special diet. Within three months, I. S. felt considerably better. Soon her metabolism and thyroid-hormone levels returned to normal. She has now maintained her weight loss for three and one-half years. She will have to continue her thyroid medication for the rest of her life.

What effect can a very underactive thyroid gland have on a child?

You have just read of a case of an adult woman with what is called adult myxedema. A grossly underactive thyroid gland can also occur in the young; it is then referred to as juvenile myxedema.

D. V. was an eleven-year-old boy who had always been well until one year before he was examined by me. At that time, he became sluggish and withdrawn, and put on sixteen pounds. As in the case of his adult counterpart, the laboratory tests showed that he was deficient in thyroid hormone. He was given the proper amount of thyroid medication to bring his hormone levels to normal, and at the same time he was placed on a well-balanced diet calculated to remove the excess sixteen pounds. This type of thyroid deficiency, juvenile myxedema, can be the result of a virus infection, or its origin may be genetic. Whatever the cause, if it is diagnosed early enough and the proper medication is prescribed, the condition is completely reversible; on the other hand, if the condition is not diagnosed and treated, brain damage will eventually occur.

I lose weight for a while and then seem to hit a plateau. Do you ever see reasons for this?

Anyone who has dieted frequently has experienced the "weight plateau." This is a condition where one loses weight regularly for several weeks or months, and then suddenly the weight losses stop and one remains at the same weight in spite of the continuing diet. In most cases, this is a temporary phenomenon, and after a few weeks one will once again begin to lose weight on the low-calorie diet; however, once in a while, the weight plateau stubbornly persists, and when this occurs, it is necessary to determine the cause of the persistent plateau.

N.W. was thirty-six years old and had experienced the Yo-Yo Syndrome of gain and loss for nine years before being examined by me. During a six-month period prior to being seen by me, she had faithfully remained on her physician's diet and had lost forty pounds, but had been unable to lose any more than that. After the forty-pound loss, she was still twenty-three pounds over her ideal weight, and had remained at this plateau for three months. Interestingly, she said that in the past, when she had started on a new diet in the winter, she had developed a bad cold.

Her laboratory tests showed that she had a deficiency of thyroxin, a thyroid hormone, and so she was placed on the proper thyroxin medication, plus a special diet beginning in the spring. Within four months, she had lost the excess twenty-three pounds.

Is there a preferred time to start to diet?

It is preferable to initiate diet programs in the spring, summer, or early fall because of the decreased incidence of respiratory infections associated with dieting during those times of the year.

Can taking medication or using medicated products affect laboratory test results?

Once in a while, accurate diagnosis of a glandular disturbance may be upset by a specific medication which a patient is taking. For this reason, it is always of the utmost importance for you to tell your physician, when asked, exactly what pills you have been taking, whether they be diet pills, sleeping pills, patent medicines, or plain aspirin. The following case illustrates, dramatically, how even simple aspirin and/or the shampoo one uses can upset laboratory tests.

L. P. was a thirty-seven-year-old woman who had suffered from the Yo-Yo Syndrome ever since the age of twenty-eight.

During this nine-year period, she had consulted twenty-seven doctors, and various clinics and hospitals in the United States and Europe; she had tried seventeen different crash diets, and had taken twenty-six different types of medication

—ranging from pills to shots to pellet implantation. L. P. had even tried surgery following hypnosis, and when that failed and she found herself forty-nine pounds over her ideal weight, she gave up on crash diets, diet pills, and the like, in despair.

A few years before being referred to me, after a period of eighteen months without pills, etc., she had a complete physical examination by a physician. She was told that her symptoms of excessive fatigue, decreased sexual interest, dry skin, brittle nails, and obesity were psychosomatic and she was referred to a psychiatrist.

The psychiatrist referred her to me for a final endocrinological and metabolic evaluation. I found that she did indeed have the above-mentioned symptoms and that her previous PBI (test for thyroid hormone) showed her thyroid to be normal.

While taking down a very detailed case history from the patient, she revealed that she used an iodine shampoo, and also was in the habit of taking large doses of aspirin. Because both of these substances are known to affect the PBI test, a more precise test, i.e., a free-thyroxin, was done. For patients taking such drugs as aspirin, free-thyroxin tests reflect thyroid function more accurately than other tests. A PBI was also done for comparison.

The PBI was reported normal because of the contamination of the shampoo and aspirin, while the more accurate free-thyroxin indicated otherwise. The low free-thyroxin coupled with her signs and symptoms clinched the diagnosis of severe hypothyroidism, or low thyroid function.

The patient was treated with the appropriate amount of thyroxin (T-4) and placed on a special diet. Within eight months, Mrs. L. P. began to feel full of life and energy; her skin lost its excessive dryness, her fingernails hardened, and she regained her former sexual desires. At the same time, she left the weight plateau she had been on and began losing, until she lost the excess forty-nine pounds.

It is now over two years since her original examination, and this patient has maintained her feeling of well-being, as well as her ideal weight of 112 pounds, without the aid of a psychiatrist.

I know there is something wrong with me but my doctor tells me I am O.K. because my thyroid test results are normal. What can I do?

It is true that a person with a normal PBI can still be hypothyroid. It is true that a person with a low basal metabolic rate is not necessarily hypothyroid. When the outward symptoms do not agree with the laboratory findings, the physician must, obviously, re-examine his findings to see if there are missing links in the symptoms, and very often, do more extensive and sophisticated laboratory testing.

S. R. was a young man of twenty-six with a five-year history of fatigue, and in addition, he was twenty-five pounds over his ideal weight. His own physician had tested him and found that his PBI and his BMR were both very low. Because of the patient's fatigue and overweight, the doctor diagnosed the condition as lack of thyroid hormone, or hypothyroidism. He then placed him on desiccated thyroid hormone. Despite the medication, the doctor noted no improvement in the patient's condition, so increased the thyroid dosage until the patient was taking fifteen grains per day. At this point, S. R. developed diarrhea, generalized shakiness, and increased nervousness.

At the onset of these symptoms, the young man was referred to me for research evaluation. I immediately took him off the thyroid medication. Blood tests showed that *he was not hypothyroid* but had a deficiency of T-B-G (a protein that binds thyroid hormone). He was also slightly anemic. He was put on a special diet and given an iron compound to counteract the anemia. At the end of four months, he had lost his excess twenty-five pounds and was no longer anemic.

For the past two years, he has been off all medication and has maintained his weight loss.

When the laboratory tests don't fit the patient's condition, you re-explore, looking for the true cause.

Could it be my glands?

The answer to the title of this chapter is "possibly"—but probably not. However, there are glandular problems which definitely do relate to obesity. The incidence is infrequent but it does exist, and in most cases, once the necessary tests are done and the difficulty is diagnosed, the condition can be corrected by proper medication.

16

The Big Debate

What is the big debate?

For more than a dozen years, a debate has been raging on both sides of the Atlantic as to the value or non-value of treating obese patients with a hormone known as human chorionic gonadotropin (HCG), plus a five-hundred-calorie diet. Although evidence on both sides of the fence is not yet scientifically conclusive, it seems appropriate to discuss the issue in view of the growing use of the hormone in the United States. It is not known how many physicians are using HCG in the treatment of obesity, but according to an article in *The Wall Street Journal* in 1970, there may be as many as four hundred. These four hundred physicians are currently using HCG on a great number of patients.

Do you recommend HCG treatment?

I *do not* endorse the use of HCG, but I do believe you should be informed as to the pros and cons of the treatment. Controlled studies have been few, and so far, the most reliable data seem to suggest that the loss of weight achieved through the treatment is due to the low-calorie diet, and not to the hormone injections. Many have suggested that the HCG is merely a placebo and its effect purely psychological. (A placebo is defined in the medical dictionary as "an indifferent substance, in the form of a medicine, given for the moral or suggestive effect.")

What is the Simeons theory of HCG?

The first use of HCG in the treatment of human obesity was by an English endocrinologist, the late A. T. W. Simeons, who treated his overweight and obese patients at the Salvator Mundi International Hospital in Rome, Italy. Almost everyone agrees that a five-hundred-calorie diet will cause a weight loss without serious ill effects, providing the diet is well balanced and contains all the necessary nutrients, and that a constant check is made by a physician to ensure that the patient's electrolyte and nitrogen balance is maintained. The controversy lies in what HCG does or does not do.

First, a look at the Simeons theory. He believed that the diencephalon, a primitive part of the brain which we share in common with all vertebrates, is the mechanism which controls the complex operation of storing and issuing fuel to the body. Because he noted that the body fat of his patients tended to be redistributed during the treatment, causing a diminution of girth even when the weight loss was small, he theorized that the daily injection of HCG triggered the activity of the diencephalon, thereby releasing stored body fat to be burned off as body fuel.

Medical science does recognize certain substances as fat-mobilizing agents. For instance, it is known that growth hormone has an effect on fat combustion, as do certain other hormones excreted by the anterior pituitary gland.

Dr. Simeons' claim that HCG is, in fact, a fat-mobilizing substance, has yet to be proved or disproved.

Is the big debate over the efficacy of the HCG treatment still continuing?

Yes, one of the most recent discussions appears in the June, 1969 issue of the *American Journal of Clinical Nutrition*. Dr. Margaret J. Albrink, a professor in the Department of Medi-

cine of West Virginia University, debates an article in the
same issue by Dr. Harry A. Gusman, from Ohio. Dr. Gusman
is a practicing physician who has used HCG for many years
in the treatment of weight problems. First, let's hear from
Dr. Gusman. He says:

> I am one of the diehards who continue to treat the
> condition [obesity] seriously. I believe that obesity is
> more than a simple disturbance of the caloric balance
> sheet and that there is a more intricate process at work.
> During the past 10 years I have been treating obesity
> with a method developed by Dr. A. T. W. Simeons that
> uses human chorionic gonadotropin (HCG). I have
> treated well over 2,500 patients of both sexes, aged 15
> to 75. Since all were private patients no double-blind
> tests or other experimental studies were undertaken.
>
> It is with consternation that I must admit I cannot
> yet fully explain why Dr. Simeons' method works. And,
> it should be noted that not everyone shares my finding
> that it does work.

Dr. Gusman believes that there are two types of fat tissue; one he calls normal, and the other abnormal. He bases
this belief, which is not shared by all members of his profession, on recent discoveries by Dr. Lester B. Salans and
his associates at Rockefeller University. Dr. Salans found
that fat cells in the obese differ from fat cells in the nonobese
in this way: those in the obese are not only more numerous,
but the individual cell is larger and seems overstuffed; furthermore, the overstuffed cells metabolize glucose (a sugar)
less efficiently than normal fat cells do.

Dr. Gusman says:

> Normal fat tissue is essential to good health and
> serves two functions, as structural material and as re-
> serve storage for fuel.
>
> Abnormal fat tissue is that accumulation, in certain
> parts of the body, from which the obese patient suffers.
> This type of fat is also a potential reserve for fuel, but
> is not immediately available in nutritional emergencies.
> Only after the normal fat reserves are exhausted will the

body yield its abnormal fat to be utilized for the emergency.

When an obese patient severely reduces his diet he first utilizes his normal fat reserves to make up the nutritional deficit. By the time the normal reserves are exhausted and the abnormal fat tissues begin to make up the nutritional deficit, the patient is already complaining of weakness and hunger while the ugly fat deposits—of which he originally wished to rid himself —have hardly been reduced. At this point, the patient often becomes depressed and frustrated, and the diet is abandoned. The increased food intake that follows soon replenishes the normal fat stores, the patient feels much better, and the overweight is perpetuated or even increased. This is probably the best explanation for the many failures to reduce weight.

Dr. Gusman goes on to discuss what he considers the validity or nonvalidity of various researchers who have experimented with the Simeons method and published their findings. The list of researchers includes both Americans and British, and the publications include reputable journals, such as the *Journal of the American Medical Association* and its British counterpart, *Lancet*. Dr. Gusman claims that many of the investigators who disclaim the effect of HCG did not follow the prescribed Simeons method to the letter. In his article, Dr. Gusman summarizes the case records of 450 patients: those who received treatment for three weeks, and those who were treated for a six-week period. In the group were eighty-one men and fifty-nine women. Their ages ranged from fifteen to seventy-five years for the men, and from fifteen to seventy-two years for the women. The average age of the men was forty-one and of the women, thirty-nine. Three hundred and twenty of the women continued the treatment for six weeks, while ninety of the men continued for the same length of time. The average weight loss for men during the six-week period was twenty-nine pounds, and for women, twenty-three pounds.

Although Dr. Gusman says it has not been possible to follow up on his patients for any extended length of time, he has reached these conclusions from his experience:

1. Ninety percent of the patients attempting to reduce their obesity were able to receive some degree of benefit of treatment;

2. About 60 to 70 percent were able to reach their desired normal weight or approximately so;

3. A majority of the patients, when asked to compare this regimen with previous forms of treatment, proclaimed this to be the easiest and most successful;

4. Many of the patients who had regained some or all of their weight claimed that they were able to keep their weight down for longer periods than previously and did not mind returning for further treatment. Some even went as far as confessing that they did not try very hard to keep their weight down because they knew that they could return and repeat their loss of weight;

5. An almost universal finding in nearly all of the patients is the "euphoria" that patients experience. This occurs in spite of the marked low intake of food. I have worked with many obese patients on diets twice the 500 calories used here and do not recall many who were happy about their situation of dieting. We do not yet have an exact explanation for the "euphoria" and the high rate of "patient acceptance" so often encountered with our method, but I cannot believe that it is due to a placebo effect or a psychological reaction between patient and physician. It is far too regular; and,

6. As in all the other methods of treatment of obesity the markedly obese show the most striking and the most satisfying results. With regulated rest periods between 6-week courses of treatment, many of these obese successfully reduced 100 lb. or more. Of special gratification are the results we obtain with those markedly obese who have accompanying diabetes mellitus of the maturity onset or stable type. Most of these patients show a marked improvement in their diabetic state as well as in their obesity. While

this is true with all forms of successful weight reduction, the improvement is more marked with HCG.

Dr. Albrink, in a guest editorial in the same issue of the journal, raises some pertinent questions. Her discussion is not a categorical denunciation but a logical set of questions which are yet to be answered. Dr. Albrink says:

> The subject resolves itself into three main parts. . . . The first is whether this treatment helps to bring about acute weight loss. The second concerns the usefulness in long-range (life-long) treatment of obesity. The final topic is the possible mechanism of action of chorionic gonadotropin in obesity. . . . Many regimens, dietary and otherwise, have been claimed enthusiastically as good treatments for obesity. Yet, there is no uniformity in the method of reporting results, and results are often reported in such a way that comparison with results of others is impossible. . . .

She takes Dr. Gusman to task, saying, "While Gusman clearly shows that his patients lost weight, he shows no quantitative comparison with other studies."

Other points Dr. Albrink emphasizes are that many methods achieve weight loss and that medical literature abounds with short-term good results. She raises the question as to whether the Simeons method does provide a more comfortable or effective method.

Dr. Albrink rightly points out that long-term results are what are really needed. She notes that although Dr. Simeons stated that seventy per cent of his patients had no relapse, he gave no figures and did not report for how long a period he continued to follow up his patients. Dr. Albrink says: "While there seems to be no objection to repeated courses of HCG treatment, would this really be feasible for a lifetime?"

As to the possible action of HCG in the reduction of weight, Dr. Albrink refers to a study made by E. Sohar in

1959, and reported in the *American Journal of Clinical Nutrition*. This investigator treated thirty-three patients with HCG, and eleven others with a placebo. Both groups were given a diet of five hundred to six hundred calories. The average weight loss in all forty-four patients was twenty pounds in forty days. He concluded that the five-hundred- to six-hundred-calorie diet was effective, but that the HCG was, in reality, a placebo, since the eleven patients who did not receive the injections of HCG lost as well as those who did.

Dr. Simeons believed that HCG in some ways makes it possible to adhere to the very low-calorie diet without discomfort. Dr. Albrink, however, points out that this claim has not been proven and, indeed, would be difficult to subject to scientific testing. She states that a good scientific theory not only is one that works but is one that can be subjected to disproof. She believes that in order to rule out ". . . the powerful placebo effect of nearly daily injections and of *daily interviews with the physician*" there would have to be psychiatric testing as well as double-blind studies to make the Simeons theory more acceptable.

Dr. Albrink also refers to studies which have shown that

> . . . except for minor fluctuations in weight due to shifts in fluid balance, neither the spacing of the meals nor the composition of the diet influences the rate of weight loss on hypocaloric [low-calorie] diets of a specified number of calories.

These studies which Dr. Albrink refers to were carried out in strictly controlled hospital metabolic-ward surroundings.

> Whether patient adherence is better on one diet than another when the patient is at home or when he has the opportunity to "cheat" has not been shown for any diet and has certainly not been shown for the combination of Simeons' specific diet with or without HCG, or with or without the daily conferences with the physicians. Therefore, the possibility still exists that his diet might be easier to follow than others, either be-

cause of something intrinsic to the diet or to the addition of HCG.

In her editorial, Dr. Albrink, very cogently and fairly, discusses the technical and scientific pros and cons of Dr. Simeons' theory and Dr. Gusman's claims and concludes:

> While many possible effects of HCG on obesity might be entertained, at the moment the burden of proof that it does anything at all is on the shoulders of its proponents. Even if some effect is conclusively shown, it will more likely be of theoretical interest rather than a practical tool for the life-long treatment of obesity. The most difficult concept for both patients and doctors to grasp is that obesity is a life-long condition that requires life-long treatment.

17

The Odd Couple

What is this "Odd Couple"?

It is maturity-onset diabetes associated with obesity. If you are not a diabetic you may wish to skip this chapter.

What is diabetes?

Diabetes is a disease that is characterized by frequent urination, frequent thirst associated with increased fluid intake, and an abnormal sugar metabolism, as manifested by an abnormal glucose tolerance. The patient may or may not have sugar in his urine, depending on the severity of his diabetes.

Are there different types of diabetes?

Yes, there are basically two different types. The type referred to above is called diabetes mellitus, which for short I will subsequently refer to as diabetes. In 1921, diabetes was thought to result from a deficiency of insulin, a hormone produced by the pancreas. In this year, Drs. Frederick G. Banting and Charles H. Best discovered the nature of insulin and its function in the human body. They found that insulin is essential to the metabolism of carbohydrates, sugar, and starches and that it makes possible, at an optimal rate, the entry of glucose into your cells. Glucose is a form of carbohydrate used by your body to produce energy, and it is stored by your liver in a form known as glycogen.

The second type of diabetes is called diabetes insipidus and has nothing to do with sugar metabolism. It concerns the loss of a pituitary hormone and the loss of water. It is not related to obesity and therefore won't be dealt with further.

Is all diabetes (diabetes mellitus) alike?

No. There are two types. One is called the juvenile type, the second is called the maturity-onset type. The patient with the juvenile type develops diabetes early in life, has a deficiency in the hormone insulin, and is dependent on insulin-replacement therapy. The maturity-onset type patient develops diabetes later in life, usually is not deficient in insulin, and can often control his diabetic symptoms by proper diet alone.

The juvenile diabetic is more often thin than fat; whereas the maturity-onset diabetic is more often fat than thin.

There are about five million diabetics in the United States, of which twenty per cent are of the juvenile type, while eighty per cent are of the maturity-onset type.

Can the fat, maturity-onset diabetic be further typed?

Yes. The fat, maturity-onset diabetic can further be divided into an obese-chemical diabetic or an obese-overt diabetic. The obese-chemical diabetic has a normal blood sugar after fasting, but an abnormal glucose-tolerance test. Therefore, members of this group may never realize they are diabetic unless they have a glucose-tolerance test.

On the other hand, the obese-overt diabetic has an abnormally elevated blood sugar after fasting, as well as an abnormal glucose-tolerance test. He is more likely to be diagnosed by his physician because of the elevated blood sugar. The "Odd Couple" syndrome is characteristic of the obese patient who also has maturity-onset diabetes, either chemical or overt.

Will losing weight help correct the symptoms of my maturity-onset diabetes?

In most (but not all) cases, the overweight or obese maturity-onset diabetic can lower his blood sugar by merely losing weight.

Did my diabetes cause my obesity or did my obesity cause my diabetes?

The theories on the relationship of obesity to diabetes are of the chicken-and-egg variety. Some medical experts believe that the obesity causes the diabetes to manifest itself, while others believe that the onset of the diabetes causes the obesity—a view obviously more likely to be popular with the obese. Since diabetes has a hereditary nature, one could conveniently place the blame on parents or grandparents.

Drs. Georgina Faludi and Gordon Bendersky of the Department of Medicine of the Hahnemann Medical College and Hospital in Philadelphia lean toward the second theory. They believe it is possible that obese individuals may have unduly sensitive insulin-producing areas of the pancreas. When these persons eat carbohydrates, such as sugar and starch, more insulin is released than is actually necessary. This excess insulin, for some peculiar reason, does not allow sugar to move quickly into the cells where it is needed. As a result, there is an accumulation of sugar in the blood. This results in high blood-sugar, which causes a lack of glucose in the nervous system, which, in turn, causes an increased appetite. When this happens, the increased intake of food causes the food to be stored as fatty tissue.

Dr. S. K. Fineberg, former Chief of the Diabetes and Obesity-Diabetes Clinic at the Harlem Hospital in New York, subscribes to the theory that "the obese patient does not become a diabetic because of his obesity. On the con-

trary, he becomes obese because he is already a diabetic."
What Dr. Fineberg is saying is that because of a predisposi-
tion to diabetes due to hereditary factors, the patient gradually becomes obese, and eventually becomes an actual
diabetic.

If I am fat and have too much insulin, *why am I a diabetic?*

It is reasonable to ask why a person who has an overabundance of insulin in the blood should have any problem
with carbohydrate metabolism. It could be that the obese
diabetic has a chemically different insulin than the non-
diabetic. Or it could be that in the fat diabetic, certain functions of the insulin become impaired. The insulin impairment
is the inability to optimally transport the energy-producing
glucose into most cells. This happens at the same time that
the insulin retains its normal function to convert carbohydrate
to turn it into fat. This promotes the storage of unwanted fat.
Dr. Fineberg believes that the primary target in diabetes is
the obesity, because weight loss usually relieves the chemical
abnormalities and the symptoms of diabetes in the obese
diabetic. He says, "It is most important for the newly discovered diabetic to see the abnormally large amount of
sugar in his urine decrease then disappear entirely as the
result of his losing ten to fifteen pounds. The proper treatment of his condition will then be firmly fixed in his mind
forever."

Will increased amounts of insulin make me fat?

Maturity-onset diabetics have trouble metabolizing or burning up carbohydrates. Recent studies indicate that obesity
affects the amount of insulin in the serum of the blood. In
addition, the amount of insulin in blood serum when the
patient is at complete rest (basal state) is directly related
to his body weight. In other words, the more insulin in your
blood serum, the fatter you are likely to be.

I like to play doctor. Can you explain to me, step by step, how my obesity, sugar, insulin and diabetes are interrelated?

From the research findings at the University of Washington School of Medicine and the Veterans Administration Hospital in Seattle by Drs. E. L. Bierman, J. D. Bagdade, and D. Porte, certain conclusions have been drawn:

1. First, in order to be diabetic you must have the genes that predispose you to diabetes;
2. Obesity is often associated with your inability normally to burn up sugar;
3. Because of your inability normally to burn up sugar, more insulin is produced as a compensatory mechanism;
4. The effect of this increased insulin production on your sugar metabolism is somewhat blunted;
5. The blunted effect of insulin on your sugar metabolism results in a decreased sugar uptake by your cells. This causes more sugar to remain in your blood;
6. Your obesity aggravates each of the above conditions, and may thus unmask genetic (inherited) diabetes at an earlier stage.

How can losing weight lessen the risk of maturity-onset diabetes?

C. G. was a fifty-year-old man, whose weight problem began when he was about forty-five years old. His waist girth had steadily grown, and by the time he sought medical help, he was forty pounds over his ideal weight.

To C. G., his weight gain was to be expected with middle age. Before he had begun to gain weight, he had attended a gymnasium once a week and swum on weekends and during the summer. When he stopped these activities, he decreased his physical exercise about ten per cent, but not his food intake. The result was a slow but steady weight gain.

Laboratory tests showed that he had a reduced glucose tolerance and insulin insensitivity. In other words, he had become what is known as a maturity-onset diabetic. In such cases the pancreas produces enough insulin, but for some unknown reason, the body is insensitive to its action and the carbohydrate is not properly metabolized. The result is stored fat. In such cases, the condition may be adjusted by a simple weight loss.

C. G. was given a simple, well-balanced, low-carbohydrate diet with enough carbohydrates so as not to endanger his health. The diet was geared to his present activity, and he and his wife began a regimen of a ten-minute walk each evening.

The result of the diet and mild exercise was a weight loss of four pounds a month, so that in one year's time, he was down to his ideal weight. For the past three years, he has kept to his recommended weight.

This case history clearly shows what you can do to help yourself lessen the risk of maturity-onset diabetes. It takes only a minimum effort as far as physical activity is concerned. As for diet, once your energy expenditure is determined by a qualified physician, it is a simple matter to adjust to a diet that will produce weight loss by taking into consideration any physical abnormalities, such as carbohydrate intolerance (inability to burn up sugar).

If I am a borderline case what is the best test to determine if I am a diabetic?

The most generally accepted testing in the diagnosis of diabetes is a glucose-tolerance test. The original studies in glucose tolerance were done on relatively young, healthy people, and these results by which we measure normal or abnormal glucose tolerance are still used as standards for all population groups, regardless of age. Scientists question whether or not a fifty-five-year-old man whose fasting blood sugar is normal but becomes abnormal after the first and second hours of the test is really diabetic, or is aging normally. They believe that in the near future the standards for glucose tolerance will be modified to reflect the differences in different age groups. Studies at the Gerontology Branch of the National Institutes of Child Health and Human Development by Drs. Nathan Shock and Ruben Andres show that we may be significantly overdiagnosing diabetes in the aged.

Is the tendency toward diabetes inherited?

Yes. We have already seen that in diabetes there appears to be an inherited factor. In popular terms, diabetes tends to "run in" families and ethnic groups.

Is there a theory to explain the evolution of diabetes?

Yes. A geneticist at the University of Michigan, Dr. James Neale, has come up with an interesting theory. He asked himself: "What does one inherit in diabetes? In families of diabetics, are they inheriting *no* pancreas, or too little insulin, or are they inheriting a substance that inhibits the action of insulin?"

The hypothesis he came up with is referred to as "Neale's Thrifty Trait." It goes like this.

> In the old days of the hunters and gatherers, food would be scarce, but when you got it you got a lot of it. Say you kill an elephant or a buffalo. Then, everybody eats like mad for a week and then there's a long stretch when there isn't any or very little food. Now, insulin has the effect of converting food into stored fat; that's one of its major physiologic actions, to facilitate laying down fatty tissue.

So Neale says

> that it would be advantageous to have an ability to make excessive insulin in a hurry, that this would be thrifty. It would also make your appetite bigger so that during the feast times one could eat more and store more fat for the lean times.

To carry his hypothesis a step further, he says that "Production of excess insulin too often could produce insulin inhibition just for your own protection."

Neale believes that what the diabetic is actually inheriting is the tendency to produce too much insulin. Subsequently, he gets in trouble with diabetes if he's in a society where food is plentiful. In short, he gets insulin inhibition to try to suppress the effect of the excess food, and that's diabetes. Dr. Neale's conjectures are only theory and have yet to be proved, but they are interesting concepts and furnish food for thought.

18

Is It All in My Head?

Can emotional problems contribute to my weight problems?

Although physiological disturbances *can* and *do* play an important role in weight control, there is little doubt that emotional problems contributes as much, if not more, to your weight problems.

The emotional problems may range from occasional nervous tension to deep-seated disturbances. You react in two ways to tension—you either eat or you stop eating. An interesting phenomenon is that thin people or people of normal weight are usually those who, under tension, stop eating, while their fatter peers tend to stuff themselves when the going gets rough.

Sometimes, when you are under tension or emotional stress due to as simple a thing as an argument with your husband or wife, worry about a child's performance at school, or other day to day irritations, you may be completely unaware of how much you are eating. For example, Dr. Allan L. Blackman, a New York physician who specializes in weight problems, says: "It's very difficult to get people to accurately list how much they eat when they have been under tension. When they start to write down exactly what they have eaten, they invariably list only a fraction. If you confront the person with the fact that she ate two pieces of cake instead of one, she will deny it; then, if you insist, saying you saw her eat the two pieces, she may counter with, 'No, I couldn't have.' The fact is that she is simply unaware that she had eaten any cake at all."

Could I be a "stress eater"?

Stress eaters are not unlike smokers who reach for a cigarette when they are upset or alcoholics who "have to have" a drink to relieve their tension. Overeating due to emotional tension is common to both men and women. Very often, there is an underlying hostility to someone or to some situation. For example, a man may feel resentment toward his boss for promoting someone over him. He may relieve his anger and frustration by overeating. A housewife may resent the fact that her husband works nights, for she feels that although she is married, she does not really have a husband. To compensate, she sits in front of the television and almost unconsciously eats her way through program after program. This often produces a symbolic chastity belt which she uses to get even with her husband.

A fat teen-ager may resent and be angered by her mother and deliberately eat two helpings of dessert in order to get even. Another group of tension eaters get up during the night and eat. Usually, the people who make midnight raids on the refrigerator do so only when they are under severe stress. Once the situation eases, the late-night eating tends to diminish.

Frequently, persons avoid coping with problems of social relationships by eating, unconsciously figuring that if they become fat they will be socially unacceptable and therefore not have to face the social situations which they fear.

Let's say a teen-age girl does not want to accept a date with a boy, either because she simply does not like him or because she is confused by her own feelings and decides she cannot face going out with him. In this situation the teen-ager may well stuff herself to the point of putting on ungainly weight, precluding the possibility of being asked for a date. If the boy still asks her out, she can always refuse by saying, "How can I go out when I look like this?"

Can you describe the "stuffing syndrome"?

Dr. Arthur Kornhaber, a psychiatrist, has described what he terms the "Stuffing Syndrome." He says that the three primary symptoms of this syndrome are constant overeating, depression, and withdrawal. Dr. Kornhaber has found in his studies two characteristic features of the chronic overeater caught in the "Stuffing Syndrome": first, increased food consumption without regard to the effect on the body, sometimes accompanied by late-night eating (he says this behavior is not unlike animals preparing for hibernation); the second characteristic feature is that the person eats without regard to actual appetite. When stuffing no longer relieves the depression, the person then uses another defense, which is *not* eating. In some instances, he may say that he eats a lot when he is just a little nervous but eats very little when he is severely troubled.

When this happens, the patient may stop stuffing altogether and become a victim of severe anorexia (the inability to eat). This condition is usually a symptom of severe depression.

Dr. Kornhaber says:

> Nocturnal stuffing supplies a sense of body fullness, and heightens the internal body perceptions of the patient. The fearful state of "nothingness" which the patient experiences prior to falling asleep is thereby avoided. The anxiety that comes with sleep and the panic engendered by the decrease in sensory input [outside influence] is the heightened internal stimuli offered by a "full stomach" in the act of digestion, in addition to unknown metabolic changes which surely do occur. The recall of early pleasant memories through active fantasy and passive "body memory" are also reassuring to the patient

Because of the stuffing behavior, the patient is able to hold tenuously to his ego. In order to function and to present a façade to the world, the patient must perform an interaction with his environment that is superficial and without reward. (For example, consider the smiling and unperturbed fat man who is also depersonalized and numb—but jolly.) When this type of person is deprived of food, his hostility and his dependency on food rise to the surface. In other words, his "self-service" system of coping with his depression has been taken away.

I am a stuffer, but always feel guilty afterward. Why do I do it?

The fat person who stuffs himself often feels guilty and shameful about his eating behavior, which he may even consider illicit. In extreme forms, Dr. Kornhaber says that ". . . there may be erotic connotations to this behavior and sexual activity may be greatly relinquished or even replaced by stuffing. This may reconstitute the pathologically vicious cycle which then further facilitates withdrawal, guilt and further regression."

Dr. Kornhaber is concerned that physicians recognize the "Stuffing Syndrome" as an early sign of severe depression, a state that may well result in the patient's inability to eat. He believes that the treatment should be on a firm and continued basis, with weekly appointments with the physician, on either an individual or group basis. He feels it is important to establish solid lines of communication and to give the patient a constant reference point. The concern and interest of the physician must be communicated to the patient. Dr. Kornhaber recommends follow-up treatment for a period of six months after satisfactory weight loss has been achieved.

Can both emotional and physical causes together cause overweight?

As we have seen, emotional problems do play an important

role in the cause of overweight and obesity, but it would be totally wrong to say that *all* weight problems are the result of emotional problems. It would be equally wrong to place all the blame on physiological causes. Very often they go hand in hand, and it is necessary to treat both the psychological and physiological disorders.

Here is a case in point and a fine example of how the problem can be conquered when the physical and psychological are treated in tandem.

Mrs. D. L. was a thirty-five-year-old housewife who had begun a spiraling weight gain over a period of three years prior to her consultation with me. At that period in her marriage she had begun to feel a lack of communication with her husband, a not uncommon cause of frustration in many marriages today. After any domestic argument she would eat to pacify her hurt feelings. She was often alone and bored and would eat to relieve her feelings.

Laboratory tests showed that she had an abnormality that physicians refer to as a blunted serum growth-hormone response to fasting. Growth hormone is produced by the pituitary gland and is responsible for body growth and carbohydrate metabolism. Because of the abnormality, the patient had high blood sugar and an impaired ability to properly burn up carbohydrate.

Mrs. D. L. was placed on an appropriate diet consisting of the proper ratio of carbohydrate to fat, a diet which was tailor-made to suit her individual needs. She was counseled as to why and when she was overeating, and her relationship with her husband was discussed. She was also advised to seek some psychiatric help, which she wisely agreed to.

Within seven months she had lost the twenty-eight excess pounds at the rate of four pounds a month. Her growth-hormone response as well as her carbohydrate metabolism returned to normal and she has maintained her ideal weight for five years.

Can a serious emotional shock cause an originally non-obese person to stuff himself?

Yes, we are all aware that serious emotional shock or trauma can cause irrational behavior. This takes various forms, depending upon the psychological make-up of the individual. Some persons become withdrawn and depressed, some find relief in alcohol, and still others find emotional satisfaction in overeating.

A.B., a forty-five-year-old man, was one who took the latter course, following his father's sudden and unexpected death. Prior to his bereavement, he had had no trouble maintaining his ideal weight.

The shock of his father's death plunged him into an indiscriminate eating pattern, and ignoring his previous adherence to good nutrition he began steadily to gain weight. He soon found himself twenty-nine pounds overweight. He complained of being fatigued, inordinately tired, depressed, and withdrawn. On physical examination, I found his left major toe to be red, hot, and swollen. This latter condition, he later told me, had been present for the past two months.

Laboratory tests showed A.B. to have an abnormally high uric-acid level in his system; he had gout. Uric-acid levels are usually abnormally high when a gout condition exists. He was placed on anti-gout medication and a low-purine diet, one low in foods that can be metabolized to uric acid. Some of the foods eliminated from his diet were liver, sweetbreads, brains, kidneys, and fermented liquors, such as wine.

His response to the treatment was dramatic but not too unusual. Within one week, the signs of gout had subsided, and within three months, his blood, uric acid, and weight had returned to their normal values.

He has now maintained his weight loss and has not had an attack of gout for three years.

What can I do to prevent my children from getting fat?

Perhaps the most important treatment for overweight and

obesity is prevention. The best place to start is with the child. It is important that children, from infancy on, should be taught good eating habits, and it is equally important that mothers should appreciate that thriving is not synonymous with excessive weight gain. In other words, a child does not have to be fat to be healthy; in fact, he may be less healthy than the lean child.

Excessive weight gain in children usually begins between seven and eight years of age. This is the period of "filling out" in the growth process. In addition, children of this age become less active due to their sitting in a classroom for the greater part of the day, and then, sitting down to do homework. For this reason, physical fitness and exercise programs should be an important part of a school curriculum. Once a child has become overweight he is obviously less inclined to exercise and so the vicious cycle begins.

In families where one or both parents are obese or inclined to overweight, it is even more important to control carefully a child's diet, since he may be predisposed to obesity because of hereditary factors. If he is taught basic nutrition and good eating habits, he may well be able to control his tendency to become fat. If heredity is a key factor in his overweight, he must face the fact that his problem is a lifelong one and needs constant attention. Very often, obesity becomes a problem of the teen-ager because of emotional disturbances of one kind or another.

Occasionally, childhood obesity may be blamed on glandular malfunction, but such cases are extremely rare. In almost every instance, the overweight may be blamed entirely on diet.

Eating habits of small children are largely developed in the home environment. Although teen-agers may pick up bad habits as their independence increases and they are allowed the freedom to congregate at the local soda fountain for the after-school milkshake, soda, or whipped-cream-laden hot fudge sundae, the pre-high-school child eats the bulk of his food at home, with occasional forays into the neighbor's cookie jar or refrigerator.

My pre-teen-ager has horrible eating habits and is growing fatter by the day. What can I do?

Sometimes a mother or father can be the cause of a child's overweight even though the parent is unaware of the fact. The child may be prodded to consume more food than he or she really wants because the parent, unconsciously, feels that encouraging the child to eat is a mark of concern and love.

The following case history will demonstrate such an example. A.N. was a pre-teen girl of nine years. She was a victim of almost too much love on the part of her mother. When her mother first sought help for her daughter's weight problems the child was twenty-five pounds over her ideal weight. Her eating habits were terrible. She constantly ate between meals, actually consuming more calories between meals than at mealtime. The pattern had developed early in life when her mother gave her sweets and candy as a reward for good behavior, and to pacify her when she hurt herself and cried.

Since most small children seek parental approval, she had become a willing member of the "clean plate" club, dutifully eating what was set before her.

A complete physical checkup revealed that the child was physically normal except for her obesity. Laboratory results, however, showed that her free fatty-acid response was diminished.

Cooperative parents helped to solve the child's dilemma. I placed her on a strict, three-meal-a-day, no-in-between-snacks diet. Her parents were admonished not to criticize her diet or to comment or tease her about her weight.

Before her consultation with me, the girl had been uninterested in any active sports and did not take part in any. Once her regimen was begun, she confessed an interest in hiking and this was encouraged.

The child proved to be a cooperative patient and lost five pounds a month. At the end of five months, she had reached her ideal weight and for the past three years has been able to maintain the correct weight consistent with her growth and development.

Why do parents encourage the "clean plate" idea?

Food as a reward is a common phenomenon, just as food is an expression of love and concern on the part of a parent. "Clean plate clubs" abound in our society. Many of our parents were members of the great immigrant society and urged us to eat because they had themselves grown up hungry and were anxious that their children not suffer the same fate. Also, deprivation of food had made them abhor waste and therefore the child was told, in effect, "waste not, want not," or heard a phrase reminiscent to many, "think of all the starving Armenians."

A number of sociologists and psychologists also attribute the "clean plate" motives to the fact that a large proportion of our parents grow up remembering the lean years of the Depression. Today, our society is generally more affluent than our parents', and we tend to be more permissive with our children providing the pocket money we never had. Thus, the path to the soda fountain and pizza parlor is cleared.

Unfortunately, in the eyes of the parents, the plump child may say to society, "see how well we take care of this child; see how much we love him; see how financially successful we have been."

There are innumerable other home influences that determine eating patterns but it is not necessary to detail all of them. One or two will suffice.

All of us have guilt feelings at one time or another in our lives. You would surely be destined for sainthood if you never did anything to give your conscience a twinge. Children are very susceptible to these guilt feelings because of their desire to please those in authority (we're not referring here to the rebellious adolescent). When mama makes a big pot of spaghetti or a rich chocolate cake and Johnny says, "I can't finish it," mama may say, "What! After mama worked so hard to make your favorite food?"

Naturally, the child feels guilty. Mama slaved over a hot stove for him and he's not showing his appreciation. In such cases poor eating habits are formed. Let's understand that overfeeding can be as harmful to your well-being as underfeeding. The roads to poor nutrition and ill health may vary but the end result can be the same: namely, a considerably shortened life span.

Is there help for me if my fatness is due to emotional problems?

Yes. The key to the successful treatment of the obese person whose overweight is due to emotional problems is the person's being able to *admit that the problem is an emotional one.* If you can come to this self-realization and seek proper professional help, the problem may well be solved, but not without your complete cooperation.

Do you recommend hypnosis and/or group therapy for losing weight?

Hypnosis has often been used by psychiatrists but with limited success. Hypnosis is not a technique to be used by unqualified persons and not every patient should be hypnotized. In some instances, hypnosis can result in severe mental disturbances which will only compound the problem. The qualified psychiatrist who has been trained in the application of hypnosis must choose his patients carefully.

Group therapy, under the direction of a competent psychiatrist or psychologist, is often very successful and there are many clinics which offer this type of treatment.

In short, *motivation* of the patients is the key word. No psychiatrist or psychologist can help the person who cannot face his own problem, or who does not sincerely wish to be helped.

19

Recent Reducing Methods

COMPUTERIZED MEDICINE—*What is it?*

Advances in computer technique now make it possible for physicians to have your weight problems analyzed by computer. There are several laboratories which provide a kit for physicians. The physician supplies the necessary blood and urine samples, other pertinent information including your medical history, returns the kit to the laboratory, and, in return, is given a computerized diagnosis. Based on this, the physician can construct a diet tailor-made for you.

CALORIE MEASUREMENT—*Is there really one?*

Yes, a "calorie meter" has been developed b Dr. Walter Bloom of the Georgia Institute of Technology. The device will enable your doctor to determine how many calories you use, so that you can adjust your eating habits to consume more or fewer calories according to whether you want to gain or lose weight. The instrument measures the volume of air you exhale, and this indicates the amount of energy you expend.

GROWTH HORMONE—*Does it affect my metabolism and weight?*

Yes, researchers have found that growth hormone probably

plays a physiological role in the regulation of carbohydrate and fat metabolism. Clinical researchers have found that obese people often have low levels of growth hormone. Dr. George Bray of Boston is conducting research into various means of raising growth hormone to stimulate weight loss. Preliminary findings indicate that large doses of T-3 (thyroid hormones) do raise GH (growth hormone) levels and weight loss ensues. These results have been corroborated by other researchers, but treatment is still considered in the experimental stage.

THYROID ANTIBODIES—*Could that be the reason why I eat normally but am fat?*

It is a possibility. Researchers have found that some obese persons produce antibodies against their own thyroid hormone. Dr. Irving B. Perlstein, an internist at the University of Louisville School of Medicine, Dr. B. N. Premachandra, an immunologist, and Dr. H. T. Blumenthal, a blood-vessel pathologist, tested 1,500 fat and thin people over a five-year period and found that fifteen per cent of the overweight subjects were chronically too fat because of some unknown metabolic defects. Dr. Perlstein said that he did not know why a person might produce antibodies against his own thyroid hormone, but genetic inheritance and stress might contribute. He said that while their thyroid glands appeared normal and tested normal, the hormone produced by the glands was not being uniformly utilized by the body. Dr. Perlstein has found that the most successful treatment is synthetic-thyroid medication to saturate the antibodies that spoil the system, and a high-protein, low-fat, low-carbohydrate diet with six to eight small meals a day.

THYROID THERAPY AND HEART DISEASE—*Is there a relationship?*

Dr. Broda O. Barnes, an endocrinologist and practicing physician in Ft. Collins, Colorado, reports success in preventing coronary disease by lowering cholesterol levels through the use of desiccated thyroid. Dr. Barnes has studied a total of 950 patients who received thyroid therapy for two to ten years—averaging five and one-half years each. Ages ranged from thirty to 101. No new cases of coronary heart disease were found during this period of observation. Dr. Barnes believes that the use of thyroid therapy alone in cases of abnormally high cholesterol levels with materially reduce the incidence of coronary artery disease. Other investigators have also reported a lowering of cholesterol levels with the use of thyroid hormones, particularly T-3.

FAT-MOBILIZING SUBSTANCE (FMS)—*Can my excess fat actually be dissolved?*

New hope for diet dropouts may be provided in the near future by the results of the research of the University of London's Dr. Alan Kekwick and the Albert Einstein College of Medicine's Dr. Eli Seifter. Both researchers, working independently, have reported a substance which dissolves stored fat in the human body. Dr. Kekwick calls it a fat-mobilizing substance (FMS). The substance is found in the urine of fasting persons. Dr. Seifter has also found that true diabetics who cannot use sugar and so draw on their own fat, and women in the fourth to six month of pregnancy also produce FMS; in the latter instance because the fetus is drawing fat from the mother's body. Dr. Kekwick has shown, clinically, that patients injected every other day with FMS, while eating one thousand five hundred calories daily, lost just over one-half pound per day. One hitch is the difficulty in obtaining sufficient quantities of FMS for large-scale programs; and another is that it is not known for how long the treatment will be effective before the results wear off.

I believe this offers a real possibility and I am designing a controlled experiment to determine whether FMS will properly take off and keep off excess weight permanently.

THE "SPARE TIRE" AND CHOLESTEROL—*Might my "spare tire" protect me from a blowout?*

The "spare tire" familiar to many a middle-aged man and woman may, in fact, be working to protect the heart by keeping the cholesterol in check. Two Canadian Professors of Medicine at the University of Toronto, Drs. Aubi Angel and Jane Farkas, have shown in animal studies that fatty tissue stores up cholesterol as well as other kinds of fat. Cholesterol in the linings of the arteries results in high blood pressure and heart attacks. Drs. Angel and Farkas explain that if the cholesterol is taken up and stored by the fat tissues—which gives one the "spare tire" look—then the arteries are protected.

WHY SOME PEOPLE GAIN WEIGHT WHEN THEY STOP SMOKING—*Is it because I then overeat?*

Not necessarily so. If you stop smoking and then put on weight you may not be eating too much after all. According to researchers at the Department of Pharmacology at the Temple University School of Medicine in Philadelphia, *when you stop smoking the metabolic rate is usually lowered and weight gain results* even if you continue to eat the same amount each day.

INFERTILITY AND OBESITY—*Is there really a chemical reason for it?*

Too fat couples, unable to have children, may have cause to blame their infertility on their obesity. Drs. Olaf Nickelsen, Rachel Schemmel, and Harold Hafs, at Michigan State University, found that ninety per cent of rats allowed to eat unlimited quantities of high-fat food became infertile, and eighty per cent of rats eating a limited quantity of high-fat food also became infertile. The Michigan nutritionists believe that high-fat body content may be associated with infertility. Our studies showed the infertile fat woman often had a corresponding abnormal hormonal problem. When the hormonal problem was corrected, so were the obesity and infertility corrected.

VITAMIN D AND THE SENIOR CITIZEN—*Should I be concerned?*

Many senior citizens, particularly those seventy years of age and over, may not be getting proper nutrition, particularly those men and women who live alone. Researchers have found that osteomalacia (a bone disease characterized by softening and bending of the bones accompanied by severe pain) is frequently due to lack of Vitamin D. According to Dr. A. N. Exton-Smith, Geriatric Consultant of the University College Hospital in London, England, the osteomalacia that they observed in the elderly was mainly due to inadequate Vitamin D in food, and lack of exposure to sunlight, leading to deficient Vitamin D synthesis of the skin. He suggests that one feasible aid in correcting the situation is the increased drinking of Vitamin D-enriched milk by elderly persons. They should also get out into the sunlight rather than avoiding it, as most elderly people do.

TOO MUCH LICORICE—*Can it be dangerous?*

A word of warning to fat, diet-prone readers. Beware of licorice as a means to reduce. Excessive quantities of licorice may produce a severe potassium depletion with acute and rapidly progressive muscle weakness and painful muscle spasms. Drs. Elliott G. Gross, James D. Dexter, and Robert G. Roth, at the Albert Einstein College of Medicine in New York, reported a case of a forty-five-year-old housewife admitted to a hospital with generalized weakness. She walked with a shuffling gait, dragging her feet, was barely able to elevate her lower limbs, and her reflexes were underactive. For the previous nine months, she had been on a fad diet, eating large quantities of licorice every day. She had been under the impression that it was highly nutritional and low in calories. Licorice contains the salt of an acid which promotes loss of potassium.

NAUSEA FROM MILK—*Could it be for real?*

If your child gets sick from drinking milk, it may be because he lacks an enzyme called lactase. Before milk can be digested, it must be broken down by this enzyme. Dr. Philip Sunshine, a Stanford University Pediatrician, has found that this enzyme lack is common among the Navaho Indians, Negroes, and Asians. Some children with this illness are thin but have a "pot belly." If you suspect it in your child, see your doctor at once.

VALUE OF EXERCISE—*Should I exercise while I reduce?*

Definitely. Our studies have shown that the more you exercise the better off you are—until a point is reached at which you would feel excessively tired. Your physician can best advise you how to gradually build up your exercising program.

SPOT REDUCING—*Can I reduce specific areas—like hips, thighs, and buttocks?*

Our studies have shown that two things are necessary in order to reduce effectively. One—eat fewer calories than you burn so that you will burn up your excess fat. Two—exercise. Orient your exercise toward those areas you specifically wish to reduce. There is no such thing as a magic pill that will specifically reduce any part of your body—like "hip pills" or "breast pills."

WEIGHT LOSS IN THE WRONG PLACES—*When I reduce I always lose an inordinate amount from my breasts, which can least afford the loss. What can be done to prevent this?*

If you lose at a rate not exceeding five pounds per month, and simultaneously do exercises that firm your breasts, you should not lose a disproportionate amount of weight from that area. Our study showed this to be true; in many cases the contour of the breasts improved because they became considerably firmer.

"SHORT CIRCUITING" OPERATIONS—*I have been told that there is a "short circuiting" operation that will result in considerable weight loss. Do you approve?*

There is significant medical controversy over the use or abuse of this kind of surgical treatment for weight reduction. The surgeon completely severs your gastrointestinal tract and reconnects it, so that you are actually "short circuited" and you don't absorb much of the food that you would otherwise absorb. Hopefully, after you reach your ideal weight a second operation reconnects you. These are not small surgical procedures; they should not be considered unless every other bona fide method of weight reduction has failed, and then only after careful consultation with your family doctor, at which time all risks will be carefully explained to you.

SURGICAL REDUCTION—*I was told I could have an operation that would cut out the fat and excess skin from my abdomen and result in instant post-surgical reduction. Do you approve?*

Not really. You should not consider this operation unless every other legitimate means for weight reduction has failed —and then only after serious talks with your family doctor. I knew of a case where the operation was successful but ten months later, after regaining much of the cut-away weight, the patient split the incision wide open. You had better be sure you won't regain weight if you decide on this one.

SEX AND OBESITY—*I have not been able physically to have sexual intercourse with my wife for the last six months because of my extreme obesity. Any suggestions?*

Yes, lose weight. However, while you are losing you certainly can enjoy a normal sex life. Use what I call the "cross technique."

Have your wife lie on her back with a pillow tucked under her buttocks and her legs spread wide apart. You lie on your right side facing toward her breasts with your hips under the arch formed by her raised legs. Your abdomen will now be to the left side of her while her abdomen will be facing up. Neither your wife's abdomen nor yours will interfere with good penetration of the penis into the vagina. The procedure works well but needs practice until it is perfected. You should burn up at least one hundred extra calories during each practice session.

After you have mastered the above technique, a simple alternative is for you to lie flat on your back with two pillows under your buttocks and have your wife sit over you, looking toward your head. Lock your hands behind your head. Your wife grasps your shoulders with her hands and pulls herself to and fro, as you move your buttocks up and down. This combination of sexual intercourse and exercise should allow each of you to burn up over 150 calories. Again, you must practice over and over again to get it just right. This is called the "right-angle reduction."

WEIGHT-REDUCTION FADS—*What are the newest fads in weight reduction? Is there anything to them?*

Recently, a popular magazine featured an article on the newest fads in weight reduction—various gadgets and pieces of clothing supposedly designed to melt away pounds and inches with a minimum of effort on the part of the wearer. Included in the weight-reduction gadgetry are slimming jeans, sauna belts and a list of "lazy" machine-type exercisers where the gadget does the work—or most of it.

You jog in place on a cushion which pushes your knees up and presumably provides as much motion as a mile of jogging; you can also jog standing still on twin platforms which alternately rise and fall; for the would-be muscle builders there is a two-pound dumbbell supposed to generate strong gyroscopic forces, so that you get as much benefit as though you were using a one-hundred-pound dumbbell.

The latest fad in this one-hundred-million-dollar-a-year business offers a method whereby you are stripp d nude, wrapped, or tightly bandaged in wet linen, soaked with a "secret formula," and finally zipped into a plastic suit. Then you lie on a couch for ninety minutes. Although actual weight is not lost there is presumably a tightening and firming of your muscles so that you look trimmer. Proponents of this method claim that fluid from fat pockets in your body is squeezed into your system and then excreted.

Sounds great if a bit torturous—the only problem is that it is medically unsound. The results are temporary, and most important of all, the wrapping method can be downright dangerous if you suffer from circulatory problems, varicose veins, or phlebitis. Certainly it should never be tried without the knowledge and consent of your own physician.

As for such things as slimming jeans, sauna belts, and the like, there is little likelihood that they do much for the person trying to melt away unwanted fat. They will make you perspire and that will result in a *temporary* loss of weight, by the scale. But if you were to check your weight several hours later, it probably would be nearly the same as it was before donning the weight-reducing gadget, unless you had not taken in any fluid at all.

Most people quickly replace lost fluid by drinking, but for some desperate, strong-minded people there can be real danger. If too much fluid is lost, and with it salt and other minerals, the effect may be the same as in heat exhaustion—collapse, coma, and even death.

Exercise is part of every physical-fitness program and is important for good health. Flabbiness *can* be conquered with proper exercise, but actual loss of body fat can only be achieved by correct eating, in the right amounts, for each person's daily energy expenditure—and that diet must be determined by the doctor, not the patient. It certainly should not be decided by the financially successful but medically untrained gadgeteer.

SELF-HYPNOSIS—*Can it help me in dieting?*

It can, if you can also talk yourself into eating a well-balanced, low-calorie diet each day.

20

Help Wanted

In this book, I have tried to outline the causes and treatment of various kinds of overweight and obesity. By now, it should be evident that the problem is a complex one and that there is no single cause. Overweight and obesity may result from simple overeating, from chemical imbalance in the body, from malfunctioning of certain organs of the body, or from mild or severe emotional disturbances. Very often, there is a combination of one or more of these causes. The trick is to *find* the *cause* and then *provide* the *treatment*. In some instances, this may be a complicated and involved process for the physician, but to obtain the desired result, one must first determine the cause, and persistence will usually win out.

Proper diagnosis in obesity, as in other medical problems, is paramount to the successful treatment, whether the causes be purely psychological or physical, or a combination of the two. Only with competent diagnosis can the cause be determined and proper treatment begun. Obviously, if the cause of the trouble is not known to the physician, the cause cannot be explained to the patient, and the hope for a cooperative patient diminishes accordingly; and cooperation between doctor and patient is a must in successful weight control!

I have presented over three dozen authentic case histories. Each one represents a different problem, although some of them may exhibit common factors. In all of the histories which are included in this book, weight reduction was successfully achieved by the patient. This does not mean that all of the patients under treatment have reached their goals, but the purpose of this book is to show that weight reduction can be attained and, even more importantly, that the ideal weight, once achieved, can be maintained.

The 50 questions following can each be answered by a "yes" or "no." It will be helpful to you and to me if you would number a sheet of paper from 1 to 50. Read each question; then answer with a corresponding "yes" or "no." After you have completed the exercise, turn to the correct answers. (Page 215.) Place an "X" after any incorrect answer and subtract the number of incorrect answers from 50.

If your score was 46–50, then you have a superb knowledge of the material in this book and, if properly motivated, your chances of a successful weight-reduction regime are excellent.

A score of 40–45 rates your comprehension of the material, as well as your chances of successful weight reduction, as good.

A score of 35–39 indicates that your knowledge and your chances of success are fair.

A score of 28–34 shows that your appreciation of this material is limited, and your chances of a successful weight reduction poor. To you, I would suggest skimming the book again.

If your score was 27 or lower then you did not grasp these concepts, and your chances of failure are probable. I recommend that you reread the book thoroughly. With better understanding, you too can be successful.

FIFTY OF THE MOST FREQUENTLY ASKED QUESTIONS
ABOUT OVERWEIGHT AND OBESITY THAT THIS BOOK
ANSWERS IN DETAIL

QUESTIONS

1. Do I have to be fat? _____

2. I eat less than my husband, but I still get fat. Is this medically possible? _____

3. Am I too fat for enjoyable sexual intercourse? _____

4. My doctor doesn't believe me when I say I don't cheat. I think I am staying on my diet. Do you believe me? _____

5. Can I reduce my hips and bosom? _____

6. Can I tell if I am too fat? _____

7. Can self-hypnosis make me lose weight without dieting? _____

8. I went on a one-thousand-calorie diet, but I still didn't lose weight. Is this medically possible? _____

9. Is exercise important? _____

10. Won't exercise only increase hunger? _____

11. Is it true that fat parents usually produce fat children? _____

12. Overweight and obesity are the same, aren't they? _____

13. If I reduce, does that mean I can never have desserts again? _____

14. Can I take off a "spare tire" around my middle? _____

15. Has Human Chorionic Gonadotropin been scientifically proven to have a beneficial effect on weight reduction? _____

16. Are fad diets really harmless? _____

17. Do you recommend a surgical operation to cut away my excess fat? _____

18. I should always start my diet in the winter, shouldn't I? _____

19. Will I probably live longer if I stay thin? _____

20. Is a fat baby always a healthy baby? _____

21. I am excessively fat and am pregnant. Should I diet? _____

22. Can teen-age skin problems be related to poor nutrition? _____

23. Does the average American get all the nutrients he needs every day? _____

24. Do I have to give up eating in restaurants in order to stay on my diet? _____

25. Can I still have a cocktail and be on a diet? _____

26. Is there such a thing as being obese non-obese? _____

27. Need I get irritable while dieting? _____

28. Can diet pills be dangerous? _____

29. I have huge legs from the knees down. Can dieting help? _____

30. Can dieting make me feel, act, and be younger? _____

31. Can fad dieting be associated with hair loss? _____

32. Can losing weight help me to become pregnant? _____

33. Do most fat diabetics have a deficiency of insulin? _____

34. Can fad diets cause me to be more forgetful? _____

35. Can "rainbow pills" lead to death? _____

36. Should I take the diet pill that worked for my neighbor? _____

37. Is it true that I can't be harmed by the macro-biotic diet? _____

38. Should diet clubs be medically supervised? _____

39. Should I see my own physician before I join a diet club? _____

40. If I have gained and lost weight all my life (the Yo-Yo Syndrome), is it possible to stabilize my weight? _____

41. My PBI blood test for thyroid is normal. Could I still be hypothyroid? _____

42. Are many of the bad effects of obesity reversible if I lose weight? _____

43. If my husband is too fat, is he more likely to have a heart attack? _____

44. Is the quality of my hair affected by what I eat? _____

45. Can losing weight help me to improve my sex life? _____

46. Can I reduce and stay that way? _____

47. Is it unusual to hit a plateau while dieting? _____

48. Can overweight or obesity be related to loss of sex drive? _____

49. Can my unborn child be affected by what I eat? _____

50. Is sexual intercourse a good form of exercise? _____

ANSWERS TO THE FIFTY MOST FREQUENTLY ASKED QUESTIONS ABOUT OVERWEIGHT AND OBESITY THAT ARE ANSWERED IN THIS BOOK

1. No	18. No	35. Yes
2. Yes	19. Yes	36. No
3. No	20. No	37. No
4. Yes	21. Yes	38. Yes
5. Yes	22. Yes	39. Yes
6. Yes	23. No	40. Yes
7. No	24. No	41. Yes
8. Yes	25. Yes	42. Yes
9. Yes	26. Yes	43. Yes
10. No	27. No	44. Yes
11. Yes	28. Yes	45. Yes
12. No	29. Yes	46. Yes
13. No	30. Yes	47. No
14. Yes	31. Yes	48. Yes
15. No	32. Yes	49. Yes
16. No	33. No	50. Yes
17. No	34. Yes	

All of the University Hospitals affiliated with the Medical Schools listed hereafter either have some form of Endocrinological and/or Metabolic Unit or they can tell you where in your area you can best receive help. For readers who would like to know the location of the medically supervised Endocrinology and/or Metabolic unit nearest to their home, the following list is supplied.

ALABAMA
  Birmingham   Medical College of Alabama

ARIZONA
  Tucson   University of Arizona, College of Medicine

ARKANSAS
  Little Rock   University of Arkansas, School of Medicine

CALIFORNIA
  Davis   University of California, Davis School of Medicine

  Loma Linda   Loma Linda University, School of Medicine

  Los Angeles   The UCLA School of Medicine

  Los Angeles   University of Southern California, School of Medicine

  Los Angeles   University of California, Irvine California College of Medicine

  San Diego   University of California at San Diego, School of Medicine

  San Francisco   University of California, School of Medicine

  Stanford   Stanford University, School of Medicine

COLORADO
  Denver   University of Colorado, School of Medicine

CONNECTICUT
  Hartford   University of Connecticut, School of Medicine

  New Haven   Yale University, School of Medicine

FLORIDA
  Gainesville   University of Florida, College of Medicine

  Miami   University of Miami, School of Medicine

GEORGIA

Atlanta	Emory University, School of Medicine
Augusta	Medical College of Georgia

HAWAII

Honolulu	University of Hawaii, School of Medicine

ILLINOIS

Chicago	Chicago Medical School, University of Health Sciences
Chicago	Northwestern University Medical School
Chicago	University of Chicago, Pritzker School of Medicine
Chicago	University of Illinois, College of Medicine
Maywood	Loyola University, Stritch School of Medicine

INDIANA

Indianapolis	Indiana University, School of Medicine

IOWA

Iowa City	State University of Iowa, College of Medicine

KANSAS

Kansas City	University of Kansas, School of Medicine

KENTUCKY

Lexington	University of Kentucky, College of Medicine
Louisville	University of Louisville, School of Medicine

LOUISIANA

New Orleans	Louisiana State University, School of Medicine
New Orleans	Tulane University, School of Medicine
Shreveport	Louisiana State University Medical Center, Shreveport School of Medicine

MARYLAND

Baltimore	Johns Hopkins University, School of Medicine
Baltimore	University of Maryland, School of Medicine

MASSACHUSETTS

Boston	Boston University, School of Medicine
Cambridge	Harvard Medical School

| Medford | Tufts University, School of Medicine |
| Worcester | University of Massachusetts Medical School |

MICHIGAN

Ann Arbor	University of Michigan Medical School
Detroit	Wayne State University, College of Medicine
East Lansing	Michigan State University, College of Human Medicine

MINNESOTA

| Minneapolis | University of Minnesota Medical School |
| Rochester | Mayo Graduate School of Medicine |

MISSISSIPPI

| Jackson | University of Mississippi, School of Medicine |

MISSOURI

| Columbia | University of Missouri, School of Medicine |
| St. Louis | St. Louis University, School of Medicine |

MISSOURI

| St. Louis | Washington University, School of Medicine |

NEBRASKA

| Omaha | Creighton University, School of Medicine |
| Omaha | University of Nebraska, College of Medicine |

NEW HAMPSHIRE

| Hanover | Dartmouth Medical School |

NEW JERSEY

| Newark | New Jersey College of Medicine and Dentistry |
| New Brunswick | Rutgers Medical School, Rutgers, The State University |

NEW MEXICO

| Albuquerque | University of New Mexico, School of Medicine |

NEW YORK

| Albany | Albany Medical College of Union University |
| Brooklyn (New York City) | State University of New York, Downstate Medical Center |

Buffalo	State University of New York at Buffalo, School of Medicine
New York City	Albert Einstein College of Medicine of Yeshiva University (Bronx)
New York City	Columbia University College of Physicians and Surgeons
Ithaca	Cornell University Medical College
New York City	New York Medical College
New York City	New York University, School of Medicine
Rochester	University of Rochester, School of Medicine and Dentistry
New York	Mount Sinai School of Medicine of the City University of New York, New York
Stony Brook	State University of New York at Stony Brook, Health Sciences Center
Syracuse	State University of New York, Upstate Medical Center, College of Medicine

NORTH CAROLINA

Chapel Hill	University of North Carolina, School of Medicine
Durham	Duke University, School of Medicine
Winston-Salem	Bowman Gray School of Medicine of Wake Forest College

NORTH DAKOTA

Grand Forks	University of North Dakota, School of Medicine

OHIO

Cincinnati	University of Cincinnati, College of Medicine
Cleveland	Case Western Reserve University, School of Medicine
Columbus	Ohio State University, College of Medicine
Toledo	Medical College of Ohio at Toledo

OKLAHOMA

Oklahoma City	University of Oklahoma, School of Medicine

OREGON

Portland	University of Oregon Medical School

PENNSYLVANIA

Hershey	Pennsylvania State University College of Medicine, Milton S. Hershey Medical Center
Philadelphia	Hahnemann Medical College of Philadelphia
Philadelphia	Jefferson Medical College of Philadelphia
Philadelphia	Temple University of the Commonwealth System of Higher Education, School of Medicine
Philadelphia	University of Pennsylvania, School of Medicine
Philadelphia	Women's Medical College of Pennsylvania
Pittsburgh	University of Pittsburgh, School of Medicine

PUERTO RICO

San Juan	University of Puerto Rico, School of Medicine

RHODE ISLAND

Providence	Brown University Program in Medical Science

SOUTH CAROLINA

Charleston	Medical College of South Carolina

SOUTH DAKOTA

Vermillion	University of South Dakota, School of Medicine

TENNESSEE

Memphis	University of Tennessee, College of Medicine
Nashville	Meharry Medical College, School of Medicine
Nashville	Vanderbilt University, School of Medicine

TEXAS

Dallas	University of Texas, Southwestern Medical School
Galveston	University of Texas Medical Branch
Houston	Baylor College of Medicine
San Antonio	University of Texas Medical School at San Antonio

UTAH

Salt Lake City   University of Utah, College of Medicine

VERMONT

Burlington   University of Vermont, College of Medicine

VIRGINIA

Charlottesville   University of Virginia, School of Medicine

Richmond   Medical College of Virginia School of Medicine, Virginia Commonwealth University

WASHINGTON

Seattle   University of Washington, School of Medicine

WASHINGTON, D.C.

Washington, D.C.   Georgetown University, School of Medicine

Washington, D.C.   George Washington University, School of Medicine

Washington, D.C.   Howard University, College of Medicine

WEST VIRGINIA

Morgantown   West Virginia University, School of Medicine

WISCONSIN

Madison   University of Wisconsin Medical School

Milwaukee   Marquette, School of Medicine

Index